ONTOLOGICAL HUMILITY

ONTOLOGICAL HUMILITY

Lord Voldemort and the Philosophers

Nancy J. Holland

Published by State University of New York Press, Albany

© 2013 State University of New York

All rights reserved

Printed in the United States of America

No part of this book may be used or reproduced in any manner whatsoever without written permission. No part of this book may be stored in a retrieval system or transmitted in any form or by any means including electronic, electrostatic, magnetic tape, mechanical, photocopying, recording, or otherwise without the prior permission in writing of the publisher.

For information, contact State University of New York Press, Albany, NY
www.sunypress.edu

Production by Eileen Nizer
Marketing by Anne Valentine

Library of Congress Cataloging-in-Publication Data

Holland, Nancy J. (Nancy Jean)
  Ontological humility : Lord Voldemort and the philosophers / Nancy J. Holland.
    p. cm.
  Includes bibliographical references (p.).
  ISBN 978-1-4384-4549-6 (hardcover)ISBN 978-1-4384-4550-2 (paperback)
  1. Humility. 2. Knowledge, Theory of. 3. Ontology. 4. Postmodernism.
5. Rowling, J. K.—Criticism and interpretation. I. Title.

BJ1533.H93H65 2012
121—dc23   2012011096

10 9 8 7 6 5 4 3 2

This one is for Jeff—
"I love you in a place where there's no space and time."

Contents

Acknowledgments	ix
Prologue: Defining Ontological Humility	1
Chapter One: Epistemological Humility and Its Other	23
Chapter Two: Ontological Humility in Heidegger	45
Chapter Three: Existential Humility and Its Other	67
Chapter Four: Postmodern Humility and Its Other	89
Chapter Five: Feminist Humility	111
Conclusion	131
Notes	135
Bibliography	145
Index	151

Acknowledgments

Many people have helped this project to move along from idea to reality. My gratitude begins with Rosa Slegers, Morny Joy, John King, and the others who heard an initial exploration of these ideas at the 2006 meeting of the International Society for Philosophy and Literature; and with Marilyn Frye, who encouraged the project in an early stage.

Since then, my thinking has benefited from the input of the enthusiastic students at the 2008 Goucher College Undergraduate Philosophy Conference; Phyllis Rooney, Nancy Tuana, and others in the audience at the 2009 Feminist Epistemology, Metaphysics, and Methodology of Science conference at the University of South Carolina; those who attended a paper drawn from this work at the 2009 meeting of the Society for Phenomenology and Existential Philosophy; and Jorella Andrews and her colleagues and graduate students who attended my 2009 guest lecture for the Program in Visual Culture at Oliver Goldsmith College, University of London.

I also thank several cohorts of philosophy majors at Hamline University who heard and commented on various stages of this project, as well as my colleagues in the Department of Philosophy there: Lisa Bergin, Duane Cady, Samuel Imbo, and Stephen Kellert. Hamline University facilitated my research on this project with a sabbatical leave in the spring term of 2010.

In addition, I am grateful for the helpful comments of two anonymous readers for SUNY Press and for the support and encouragement of my editor, Andrew Kenyon, and his predecessor, Jane Bunker.

Finally, I have to acknowledge two people without whom this work literally would not have been possible: my husband, Jeffrey Koon, who patiently read and commented on every chapter (the Heidegger chapter twice), and of course, J. K. Rowling, who created Harry Potter and his world.

Prologue

Defining Ontological Humility

In the Beginning

> ... [I]t would be strange to think that the art of politics is the best knowledge, since man is not the best thing in the world.
>
> —Aristotle, *Nicomachean Ethics*

This book explores the concept of "ontological humility," as developed from the work of twentieth-century German philosopher Martin Heidegger, and traces its role in philosophical thought from the seventeenth century to contemporary gender and race theory. While some recent scholarship in both philosophy and feminism points indirectly to this concept, it has not yet been named or systematically explored for its potential value in a range of fields, from epistemology and ethics to the protection of our environment and the understanding of oppression. The goal of this book is to demonstrate how ontological humility not only generates better philosophy, but might also show us how to lead better lives and how to live in a way that allows others to lead better lives as well.

The initial argument is that the moral worth of Harry, Dumbledore, and others in J. K. Rowling's Harry Potter stories is due to their humility in the face of the magic that was given to them and which enables them to be the witches and wizards that they are. Voldemort and his "Death Eaters," conversely, are marked by their arrogance, their certainty that they deserve the power they have and that those who lack it are inferior. Voldemort, moreover, is motivated by what Rowling suggests is the ultimate arrogance, the desire to conquer death, while it is Harry and Dumbledore's willingness to die that finally defeats the Dark Lord.

The key to ontological humility lies in understanding that the same life options are open to "muggles," too, and that many philosophers over the last four centuries have shared that belief. We are where we are, with the resources and liabilities we have, surrounded by a particular group of others like ourselves, because these things have been "given" to us by what Heidegger calls "Being," in the same way that magic has been given to Harry Potter. We can believe that we deserve them because of some inherent or achieved virtue of our own, but whatever we might have done to merit our success in any endeavor owes far more to chance, or fate—this being "given"—than it does to our own efforts. Once one is convinced of this, a whole set of ethical imperatives is revealed that greatly narrows the range of morally valid options with regard to many of the major social and political issues of the day.

As we will see, I find this theme throughout Heidegger's work, but will focus for now on the connection he makes between the German words for "to send" (*schicken*), "history" (*Geschichte*), and "destiny" (*Geschick*). Heidegger relates this linguistic triad to how the world we live in and our place in that world is shaped, if not determined, by forces we can neither control nor completely understand. In his "Letter on Humanism," he also links history and destiny to the "*es gibt*" (literally, "it gives," but the German equivalent of "there is"), and to the world as "given" to us, rather than of our own making. One can, thus, see his criticisms of Jean-Paul Sartre's version of existentialism in the "Letter" as based, among other things, on Sartre's disregard for the contingencies of human life and the limits of human understanding. As opposed to Sartre's assertion of human defiance in the face of Being, Heidegger, I will argue, champions ontological humility.

The concept of ontological humility also offered an unexpected insight into why the work of some figures in twentieth-century European philosophy (Heidegger, Maurice Merleau-Ponty, Jacques Derrida) held my interest, while that of their close intellectual allies (Sartre, Albert Camus, Michel Foucault) did not. And the same held true for philosophers in the so-called modern period (1600–1800). What provided the immediate catalyst for this book, however, was the realization that the Harry Potter saga, which I had been reading to and with my children almost since its inception, embodied the same kind of "ontological humility" that I found in Heidegger and others. Convinced that the theoretical and practical implications of the concept for living well and creating a better world were worth exploring more fully, I knew I could not pass up the gift J. K. Rowling had unintentionally given me. This book is the result of the destiny that links Lord Voldemort to the philosophers.

Lord Voldemort and the Philosophers

"Trivial hurts, tiny human accidents," said Firenze, as his hooves thudded over the mossy floor. "These are of no more significance than the scurrying of ants to the wide universe. . . ."

—*Harry Potter and the Order of the Phoenix*

I

As is well known, the British edition of the first of Rowling's Harry Potter books is *Harry Potter and the Philosopher's Stone*. The U.S. publishers changed the title to *Harry Potter and the Sorcerer's Stone,* perhaps because they thought American readers wouldn't know what the philosopher's stone was, or perhaps because they feared the word *philosopher* would scare readers away. It is, in any case, an interesting alchemy to turn philosophers into sorcerers. In this section, I will go back along the path created by this alchemy from sorcerers to philosophers.

First, however, it is necessary to acknowledge the existing body of philosophical literature on the Harry Potter books, including significant critiques from the perspectives of class, race, gender, and postcolonial thought, as well as critiques that highlight the relative invisibility of lesbian, gay, bisexual, transgender, and intersex (GLBTI) characters and the author's reliance on violence to resolve conflict. I won't duplicate any of that thinking, but will use the Harry Potter saga to illustrate a different kind of philosophical thought, so different that it lacks a commonly recognized name. Still, its roots spread across a wide range of the philosophical literature, from eighteenth-century philosopher David Hume's "mitigated skepticism"[1] to nineteenth-century theologian Søren Kierkegaard's "infinite resignation"[2] to contemporary feminist Marilyn Frye's "loving eye."[3]

I have labeled this way of thinking "ontological humility." Why "ontological"? Since philosophers talk about the kind of questions addressed here much more often than most people, they have developed their own vocabulary for doing that. The literal meaning of "ontology," from ancient Greek, is "the science or study of Being," of what it means to exist. This field of philosophy examines questions such as what it means to say that something (a unicorn, for instance, or democracy) does or doesn't exist, either in general or at a specific time and place. It also looks at whether all the things we commonly assume do exist—from humans and nation states to atoms and stories—exist in the same way, and in what sense, if any, things like numbers and pure geometrical figures can be said to exist at all.

Ontological humility, then, is meant to describe humility in the face of Being, that is, humility in the face of the unknowable whatever that is responsible for the fact that we exist, and that also explains how and why we exist. The most important and perhaps the only thing we know about Being in this sense is that it is transcendent to human experience. This means that it affects our lives, but exceeds anything we can ever know about it, thus seeming to come from beyond, or transcend, the human world. Gods and religious experience are generally understood to be transcendent in this way, but so are many other features of human life.

Some more mundane transcendentals are relatively easy to understand. Transcendental numbers such as pi are numbers that can be mathematically resolved only at the point of infinity. The concept of infinity is itself transcendental, not only because it is inconceivable, but also because it is what philosophers call a "condition for the possibility" of some kinds of mathematics, such as calculus, but not a direct object of study for them.

At another level, time and space can be said to be transcendental because we can experience, or even imagine experiencing things, only in some spatiotemporal context, but some philosophers would argue that we don't experience time and space themselves. They argue that time and space are the conditions of the possibility of our experience, but not part of our experience. For Hume, the same is true for the concept of causal necessity. For other philosophers, morality is transcendental because it is independent of the conditions of human existence, that is, it doesn't take into account what human beings may want or need—for Immanuel Kant, we can never lie, even to save a human life, because lying is always wrong.

The transcendence of Being is much harder to explain, so rather than try, I am going to the use the unnamed source of the magic that gives Lord Voldemort and the other witches and wizards in Harry Potter's world their power as a placeholder for this transcendence. In Rowling's books this unknown source of magic entails a clear set of rules (or morality) for using magic,[4] and demonstrates occasional randomness in bestowing it (e.g., the existence "mudbloods," or witches and wizards born into nonmagical families, and "Squibs," people with no magic born into magical families). These traits make the source of magic a useful metaphor for Being. At the same time, as suggested above, Rowling's story illustrates quite clearly what I mean by humility in the face of that Being.

As already noted, the more philosophical basis for my thinking here can be found in the work of Martin Heidegger, who believes that the German *es gibt* (there is) names Being's "giving" of what exists.[5]

For Heidegger, this means that we are given, or sent, a history that is also a destiny or fate, as Harry is destined to destroy Voldemort. We'll look into this in more detail later, but the important thing here is that the attitude that Heidegger seems to recommend toward this giving or this gift is something very much like humility.

In the Harry Potter stories, the source of magical power, whatever it is, can serve as a placeholder for Heidegger's "it gives." Using this interpretation, it could be said that Harry was "given" his unusual powers when Voldemort tried to kill him. And in the same moment, ironically, because Voldemort tried to defy the fate he believed was decreed by a prophecy, that is, because of his lack of ontological humility, he sealed his own doom.[6]

II

I would argue that the contrast between humility and arrogance is, in fact, the basic dynamic of the Harry Potter saga. Arrogance marks not only Voldemort but also the Dursleys, Harry's "muggle" (nonmagic) foster family, as well as Dolores Umbridge and others at the Ministry of Magic who aren't directly followers of the Dark Lord. Interestingly, it also marks as evil Draco Malfoy's mother and other parents among Voldemort's Death Eaters, despite their genuine love for their children, as Mrs. Malfoy reveals in the opening scene of *Harry Potter and the Half-Blood Prince*.[7] Perhaps most significantly, Snape's memory of something Harry's father, James, once did disturbs Harry so much in *Harry Potter and the Order of the Phoenix* that he runs a great risk to talk about it with Sirius Black, who confirms Snape's memory and describes himself and James Potter when they were students at Hogwarts as sometimes "arrogant little berks."[8]

Conversely, humility in the face of magic power appears not only with unalloyed goodness, as in the characters of Dumbledore and Professor McGonagall, but also with a less elevated openness to a power beyond oneself. To take just three examples, consider the Unbreakable Vow Snape takes that ties his fate to Draco's;[9] the scene in *Harry Potter and the Half-Blood Prince* in which Fleur is transformed from an object of derision to a sympathetic character when she proves the genuineness of her feelings for her now badly disfigured fiancé;[10] or Harry's decision in *Harry Potter and the Deathly Hallows* to "continue along the winding, dangerous path indicated for him by Albus Dumbledore, to accept that he had not been told everything that he wanted to know, but simply to trust."[11]

These examples, however, suggest one potential misunderstanding of ontological humility. A colleague responded to the title of this project by suggesting that arrogance in our ancestors might have been an evolutionary advantage, but this confuses arrogance or humility as personality traits with ontological humility. As we will see, arrogant philosophers may easily be humble human beings and, more commonly, arrogant human beings may understand ontological humility. What I mean by arrogance is *not* the virtue of pride in Aristotle, sometimes translated as "high-mindedness," that is, thinking oneself "worthy of great things, being worthy of them," a trait entirely compatible with ontological humility that one also finds, for instance, in Dumbledore. (It perhaps should be said that, even for Aristotle, the vice in opposition to this virtue is "undue humility," not humility per se.[12]) What I mean by arrogance is not this pride, but something closer to Aristotle's vice of ambition or "honor-loving": "We blame the ambitious man as aiming at [being honored] more than is right and from the wrong sources" (1125b). Rather than earn Dumbledore's esteem and respect, for instance, Voldemort chooses to demand something approaching worship from those he can easily dominate.

But the real clue to my meaning can be found in my earlier reference to Heidegger. I would define "arrogance" as the denial of the contingency of human life and of our dependence on the world that we have been given. Such arrogance resists the idea that we are neither "the best thing," as Aristotle says, nor, to use Heidegger's metaphor, potentially omniscient observers of a "world picture," one characteristic of which is "loss of the gods,"[13] that is, of any transcendental power. In Voldemort, this arrogance takes the form not only of considering himself "the greatest sorcerer in the world"[14] (which might be considered only Aristotelian pride), but more importantly, it takes the form of attempting to achieve immortality: "You know my goal—to conquer death."[15] Conversely, as we have seen, it is Harry's willingness to die in *Harry Potter and the Deathly Hallows* that saves him.[16]

Voldemort's arrogance is closely linked to, but not identical with what Rowling acknowledges in an interview on the DVD of *Harry Potter and the Chamber of Secrets* is the overt moral message of her work—the "racism" embodied in the terms "pure blood" and "mudblood." One distinction between Voldemort's arrogance and the arrogance of Harry's father and Sirius in their youth (who befriend a werewolf) is Voldemort's emphasis on the bloodlines of those he leads or opposes, or at least his manipulation of such arrogance in his followers, one of whom refuses to believe Harry when he tells her Voldemort himself is only "half blood."[17] This same "racism," in the form of Voldemort's distain for goblin and house-elf magic, is what opens the way for his defeat. But "racism," while important, seems to me less central to the stories than the arrogance that claims virtue or power based on the contingencies of blood and birth.

In fact, Rowling appears explicitly to manipulate the antithesis of arrogance and humility. She creates, for instance, matched pairs of characters that seem to be based on this opposition, such as Sirius, whose arrogance borders on evil, and Remus Lupin, who is one of the saga's heroes despite being a werewolf. Another such pair is Hagrid, the half-giant gamekeeper who does a good deal of harm, but is redeemed by his recognition that he is only a "half-blood" with limited magical skills, as opposed to Filch, the caretaker, who is a Squib, and his arrogant abuse of his role at Hogwarts and refusal to accept that he will never be able to do magic. It is also notable that the ambiguous character of Snape evidences both signs of arrogance (especially in the first book) and humility (increasingly as the series goes on), which makes it more difficult for readers to be certain of his moral status until the final chapters of the saga.

III

What has become of the philosophers here? They can perhaps be seen most clearly, appropriately enough, in *Harry Potter and the Sorcerer's Stone*, when Professor Quirrell, who has been possessed (for want of a better word) by the temporarily disembodied Voldemort, says of himself before he met the Dark Lord, "A foolish young man I was then, full of ridiculous ideas about good and evil. Lord Voldemort showed me how wrong I was. There is no good and evil, there is only power, and those too weak to seek it."[18] Rowling seems to invoke Friedrich Nietzsche's words here, rightly or wrongly, as shorthand for the nihilism of what some philosophers call "modernity."

Modernity is not itself evil. The Ministry of Magic, for instance, represents the (initially) benevolent, bureaucratic side of modernity. Still, without the Ministry's unwitting support, Voldemort would have no chance of success. Rowling represents another aspect of modernity in the statue in the Ministry of Magic's lobby that represents a centaur, a house elf, and a goblin looking up adoringly at a witch and wizard.[19] This recurring image implies that Rowling is concerned with human arrogance not only toward our own origins and fate, or toward each other, but also toward those with whom we share the planet. She sometimes faintly echoes Heidegger's claim in "Letter on Humanism" that "Man is not the lord of beings. He is the shepherd of Being." Voldemort might not care much about that distinction, but in his search for power he might care very much about what Heidegger goes on to say: "Man loses nothing in this 'less'; rather, he gains in that he attains the truth of Being" (BW 245).

Heidegger, in another famous quotation, also said "Only a god can save us." By this, I think, he meant that the solution for the dilemmas of his age, and ours, will not come from us, but will be "given" or "sent" to us, just as Harry Potter was "sent" to his world (unwittingly by Voldemort himself) to defeat the Dark Lord. In our world, Heidegger calls the transcendence that might send such a god "Being." What I hope to show in what follows is that a wide range of other philosophers over the last four hundred years have shared his belief in this "Being," using many different terms for it, and have argued, albeit indirectly and often obscurely, that the proper attitude to take toward such this transcendence, however it might be understood, is a humility that reflects both its total independence of human will and our total dependence on it.

Indeed, once one starts looking for ontological humility, it shows up in philosophical writings of all sorts, even those that seem the most removed from Heidegger's thought, or Harry Potter's world. In reading some of these other philosophers, we can learn two more important things about ontological humility. One is that it has an intrinsic link to contemporary feminist thought. Another is that ontological humility must be distinguished from what might seem to be its parallel in the religious sphere. Despite Heidegger's "only a god can save of us," I will argue that ontological humility can be understood and lived—perhaps better understood and better lived—outside of a religious context. First, however, I will provide a preliminary sketch of why feminism is inherent in any form of ontological humility.

The Arrogant Eye and the World Picture

> But we also think that what distinguishes the tyrant from the man of good will is that the first rests in the certainty of his aims, whereas the second keeps asking himself, "Am I really working for the liberation of men? Isn't this end contested by the sacrifices through which I aim at it?"
>
> —Simone de Beauvoir, *The Ethics of Ambiguity*

I

In a 2006 "Musing" in *Hypatia: A Journal of Feminist Philosophy*, contemporary Canadian philosopher Lorraine Code talks about the value of what she calls Continental philosophy for the feminist philosophical project because of Continental philosophy's constructive form of skepticism and its greater openness to ambiguity than most Anglo-American philosophy.[20] What does Code mean by "Continental" philosophy? After all, as Cuban-American philosopher Ofelia Schutte has pointed out, there is more than one continent. The geographical counterpart to Continental philosophy Code uses above is Anglo-American philosophy (meaning English-language philosophy) but both these terms are misplaced shorthand. The real difference here is neither geographical nor linguistic, but genealogical, as reflected by Code's preferred term for her own tradition, "analytic philosophy."

Although dividing up the philosophical world along the English Channel has roots that go back to roughly the twelfth century, in its modern form it reflects the difference between philosophers (mostly Latin American and European, with French and German variants) who take Kant's attempt in the eighteenth century to reshape the philosophical world seriously and those (mostly from the English-speaking world) who do not.[21] This is where the term "analytic" comes in. For those who regard Kant as simply and perhaps obviously wrong, the most viable alternative to what they consider his retreat to a prescientific metaphysics is for philosophy to focus its effort on the analysis of scientific method (with its proven ability to discover truth), and of language and logic (which tells us how to preserve truth). This is the view of Hume, for instance, the philosopher who spurred Kant to new philosophical heights (or depths, depending on your perspective).

Twentieth-century British philosopher A. J. Ayer tells us that the role of philosophy is to "clarify the propositions of science by exhibiting their logical relationships, and by defining the symbols which occur in them."[22] Beyond the scientific realm, Robert Ammerman says that analytic philosophers are "interested in analyzing linguistic or conceptual units . . . to understand the structure of language by a careful study of its elements and their interrelations."[23] Analytic philosophers generally deny the existence of transcendentals like the Good or the True. They study "truth" by looking at what it means to say that a sentence is true, and approach ethics by looking at how we use the word "good."

This is the philosophical version of the rejection of transcendence that is characteristic of "modernity," and it has its own forms of arrogance and occasional humility. Other than Hume's work, however, we won't be looking at analytic philosophy in any depth here, for the reasons Code suggests: from the perspective of ontological humility, most analytic philosophy has insufficient respect for skepticism and the irreducible ambiguity of human experience, for our need to accept, as Harry Potter learns to accept, that we have "not been told everything that [we] wanted to know."[24]

So far, though, Code hasn't really said anything new. Many feminists who work in the Continental tradition have made the same point over the last quarter century or so. Even other feminists who work in the analytic tradition, such as Naomi Scheman, have made similar arguments.[25] As Code notes, however, such work has primarily focused on "ways of thinking *from* Continental *to* analytic philosophy" (SLA 223, her emphasis), with little consideration of what might be found if we moved in the opposite direction, from analytic philosophy to the work of someone like Heidegger.

What struck me about Code's restatement of the issue was the way it echoed my thinking about ontological humility. She sets the value of skepticism and the usefulness of ambiguity against what she calls "the quest for certainty" characteristic of "post-positivist [i.e., analytic] epistemologists and ethical-political philosophers, at least since the early twentieth century" (SLA 222). Thus, her article suggests that resources for understanding ontological humility might be found in Anglo-American feminism, as well as in the work of thinkers in the so-called Continental tradition.

Code's article, along with a chance encounter with Marilyn Frye, led me to reread a key text of second-wave feminist philosophy—Frye's "In and Out of Harm's Way: Arrogance and Love." My initial interest was in Frye's discussion of arrogance, but I quickly found that this article resonates on many levels with Heidegger's work. This despite Frye's roots deep in Anglo-American philosophy and her focus in this article on the need for "a radical feminist vision" (AL, 52), a project that cannot in any sense be seen as Heideggerian. Frye's article is, like all philosophy, a product of its time, but her description of "the arrogant eye" offers one model of how we might think *from* analytic philosophy *to* Heidegger, and demonstrates the intrinsic connection between ontological humility and contemporary feminist thought.

II

Frye makes several arguments in her article, some of which are no longer fashionable, if not simply wrong. Others, however, remain as current as the Harry Potter books themselves. One of those is her claim that the ideology underlying contemporary American society structures and facilitates the exploitation of women, whether that is intentional on the individual level or not. She argues that what she calls the "arrogant eye" "has the support of a community of arrogant perceivers, among whom are all or most of the most powerful members of the community at large," and it is regarded as " 'normal' perceiving among those who control the material media of culture and most other economic resources" (AL 72). This has not changed as much as we might like to think. Even Rowling, who gives Harry Potter a female friend far more intelligent than he is, also creates a magical race of females called Veelas, beautiful witch/sirens who serve as cheerleaders at a Quidditch match to distract male players on the other team (and the referee).[26]

Part of why "the arrogant eye" continues to govern many aspects of our culture may lie in another of Frye's arguments: that Western philosophy in the modern period lies at the base of this masculinist ideology, so that refuting and restructuring the one demands the refutation and restructuring of the other. (Frye herself does not limit the discussion to the modern period, but Susan Bordo makes a strong argument that earlier formulations of the relationship between men and women/nature worked in significantly different ways, and her discussion has important similarities to Heidegger's account of the uniqueness of the modern age.[27]) While our discussion here will allow us to make distinction between philosophers who evidence ontological humility and those who do not, the popular understanding of science and philosophy clearly sees them both as paradigmatic cases of the arrogant eye.[28] They, and their practitioners, are seen, not unlike Lord Voldemort, as understanding "everything that is [as a] resource for man's [or wizards'] exploitation" (AL 67). This arrogance applies equally to the natural environment, including animals, and to women and other oppressed people. (Remember the statue in the Ministry of Magic.)

Frye also describes the manipulations—genetic, physical, and behavioral—needed to adapt an animal such as a draft animal for human use as a "tool," that is, an animal "so constituted and shaped that it is suited to a user's interest in bringing about a certain sort of effect." Animals used as a resource, on the other hand, must be transformed to be put to use, as cattle are when used as meat (AL 57–58). She argues that exploitation and oppression are how humans adapt other humans as tools for their use, balancing the dehumanization of their objects with the manipulation of their uniquely human abilities. Again, this echoes Lord Voldemort's plans for the world, but obviously for Frye it is not accomplished through magic, but through a psychological process in which the exploited person comes to see the well-being of her oppressor as identical with her own. This, in turn, agrees with the perception of those whose "arrogant eyes . . . organize everything seen with reference to themselves and their own interests" (AL 67).

Whatever position one might take on whether this remains, or ever was, true on the individual level, that it works roughly as Frye describes it on the societal level can be proven simply by turning on a television set. Her analysis of the situation of the natural world, animals, women, and others in the scope of the arrogant eye also has clear links with Heidegger's account of our technological age in which "everything is ordered to stand by, to be immediately at hand, indeed to stand there just so that it may be on call for a further ordering" as what he calls a "standing reserve" (QT, 17).

At first glance, Frye's emphasis on women as the paradigm for objects of arrogation for literal men might seem worlds away from Heidegger's concern about the hydroelectric dam across the Rhine River and "the vacation industry" (QT 16). But compare Frye's above definition of the arrogant eye with how Heidegger characterizes modernity in "The Age of the World Picture": "Man becomes that being upon which all that is, is grounded as regards the manner of its Being and its truth. Man becomes the relational center of that which is as such" (QT 128). Whether as tool or resource, the natural world is what man defines it to be. And a breed of animals', or women's, "true" nature is defined in terms of their suitability for furthering the ends of those men who control technology.

Thus, Frye opens Heidegger's text to a constructive rereading.[29] Her text underscores, for instance, the extent to which the word "man" in Heidegger's writing is not an inadequate translation of the neuter German noun *das Mensch*, people in general, but reveals the gender-specific meaning hidden in Heidegger. Beyond his own reservations about the use of the word "humanism" for his thought,[30] it is not humanity as such that is "the relational center of that which is" in modernity, but rather that narrow segment of humanity at the center of technology, a segment that is, in fact, overwhelmingly white and male, and traditionally characterized in terms almost identical with those that define the masculine in Eurocentric culture.[31]

Frye's work can also reveal that what Heidegger, perhaps disingenuously, considers the "danger as such" of a (future) "precipitous fall" in which humanity itself would be "taken as standing-reserve" (QT 26–27) is how too many people already live (and many more were forced to live under the Third Reich). Too many women, and men live in a world structured so that their "pursuit of [their] own survival or health and [their] attempt to be good always require, as a matter of practical fact in the situation, actions that serve [the powerful]" (AL 70–72). Too many people worldwide are seen by the arrogant eye to exist only to serve as "standing reserve" for those who control technology, as surely as the airplane on the runway.[32]

Frye's article, however, is much more than an implicit critique of Heidegger. Both thinkers argue that the problem is not just a relatively benign matter of how "man" looks at "his" world and those who share it, something that might be resolved by correcting a minor philosophical error. Frye says, "The arrogant perceiver falsifies . . . but he also coerces the objects of his perception into satisfying the conditions his perception imposes" (AL 67). More importantly, she goes on to say that

> If someone believes that the world is made for him to have dominion over and he is made to exploit it, he must believe that he and the world are so made that he *can*, at least in principle, achieve and maintain dominion over everything. But you can't put things to use if you don't know how they work. So he must believe that he can, at least in principle, understand everything. (AL 71, her emphasis)

As we will see, for René Descartes, a tree can't become an Aristotelian unfolding of some innate essence, because we cannot know that essence.[33] From his scientific perspective, the tree becomes nothing more than what we can know it to be, a resource for providing humans with wood, shade, and so on.

This is why to question the status of women in the modern world is to question the underlying assumptions of that world itself. The reverse also holds: to question, as Heidegger does, the underlying assumptions of modernity is to question the status of women in the modern world. Even the most sexist of male thinkers (a category Heidegger arguably falls into) cannot evade this implication of their work if they undertake a thoroughgoing philosophical critique of modernity, which is why, at least for those of us raised in the shadow of Anglo-American philosophy, Frye's feminist thinking can shed light on Heidegger.

III

Frye's account, for example, clarifies why, for Heidegger, science serves technology, rather than the other way around. It is the need to be able to exploit the natural, animal, and human worlds that governs the drive for the knowledge necessary to do so. Heidegger's explanation is similar but, typically, must less direct: "But physical science does not first become research through experiment; rather, on the contrary, experiment becomes possible where and only where the knowledge of nature has been transformed into research" (QT 121). We have learned from the work of Thomas Kuhn and others that the systematic study of natural processes can take other forms than those we know as "exact" science.[34] It is the underlying attitude toward the natural and human worlds that defines modernity.[35] As Heidegger says, technology "happens to think of putting exact science to use" only because it "put to nature the unreasonable demand that it supply energy that can be extracted and stored as such" (QT 14), as a standing reserve that exists in quantifiable ways amenable to mathematical calculation and manipulation.

Frye's account of the arrogant eye's opposite, "the loving eye," can also enrich our understanding of ontological humility. "The loving eye knows the independence of the other. It is the eye of a seer who knows that nature is indifferent . . ." (AL 75). She gives an account of what life might be like for women "not pressed into a shape that suits an arrogant eye." She does not mean by this "a specious absolute independence" from the existing society, because language and meaning are social in nature. Thus, she exhibits a certain humility, as we will see Heidegger does, with respect to our dependence on a common social life to be the beings that we are. She understands that the radical social change she works for threatens to lead us "to that edge of the world where language and meaning let go their hold on our lives" (AL 76–78). This is why she emphasizes the need for feminist community to provide an alternative social context in which to bring such change about. Only "under the gaze of a loving eye" can a woman "experience directly in her bones the contingent character of her relations to all others and to Nature," a future for which Frye says we must "wait, and see" (AL 82).

While far more personalized than Heidegger's account, this is in many respects the same attitude he recommends for those who attempt to counter the power of technology and its demand for a standing reserve. (And the same attitude Harry Potter finally takes to the tasks assigned to him by Dumbledore.) Heidegger suggests that we seek a "saving power" in the midst of the danger itself: "Through this we are not yet saved. But we are thereupon summoned to hope in the growing light of the saving power. How can this happen? Here and now and in little things, that we may foster the saving power in its increase" (QT 33). (Remember here the dozens of little guerrilla actions the Hogwarts students in Dumbledore's Army undertake in *Harry Potter and the Deathly Hallows* to make Harry's final victory possible.)

What Heidegger brings to Frye's vision, then, is a much wider scope and at the same time a much more detailed analysis of the origins and dangers of modernity for all of us. Perhaps more significantly, however, what Frye brings to Heidegger is the urgent reminder that not all of us live that danger in the same way and from the same location. Further, the parallels between her work and Heidegger's suggest that the "little things" that foster the saving power must include, if not focus on, those things that would restore to those who already live their lives as standing reserve a fully human existence and the freedom to engage for themselves in that questioning that Heidegger tells us is "the piety of thought" (QT 35). Thus, despite Heidegger's own declarations and intentions, the critique of technology that is central in his later work cannot be other than a political project, just as it cannot be other than an exercise in humility.

The Wizard of Infinite Resignation?

> So that, upon the whole, we may conclude, that the *Christian Religion* not only was at first attended with miracles, but even at this day cannot be believed by any reasonable person without one.
>
> —David Hume, *An Enquiry Concerning Human Understanding*

> Faith is a marvel.
>
> —Søren Kierkegaard, *Fear and Trembling*

I

Before moving on, it may be necessary to remind ourselves that ontological humility, in the sense I use the term here, is what might be called an "intransitive" humility, a humility without anyone or anything before which to humble yourself (which is why I prefer it to Nietzsche's "gratitude," which implies gratitude toward someone or something). While ontological humility acknowledges Being, that is, something that transcends our experience and is its source, it is central to my argument that Being is not sufficiently specific or personal to be defined as a god or God in any recognizable sense.

I've already cited Heidegger's famous "only a god can save us," and claimed that this late dictum alone is not sufficient grounds to claim any theological (or onto-theological, to use Heidegger's term) significance for Being. I will explain this claim more specifically with regard to Heidegger in chapter 2. Here, I will make the argument in a briefer form, ironically by drawing on the work of one of the foremost religious thinkers of the last two centuries, Søren Kierkegaard, whose work had a profound influence on Heidegger's thought.

The aspect of Kierkegaard's work that I will focus on is the distinction he makes between "the Knight of Infinite Resignation" and "the Knight of Faith." In his work, these are the last two stages of human aspiration. The first two stages, most famously described in *Either/Or*, are the Aesthetic and the Ethical. The Aesthetic or preethical life is probably best represented by the great Romantics who were Kierkegaard's contemporaries. The Ethical life is one that embodies the morality taught by G. W. F. Hegel's nineteenth-century Danish followers.[36] For Kierkegaard, the Aesthetic life can be one of amoral pleasure (hence, "The Seducer's Diary" in *Either/Or*), but its distinguishing feature is not so much the search for pleasure per se as a life lived with no relationship to God, a life devoted to the pursuit of inchoate emotions unimpeded by either reason or morality. There are elements of the Aesthetic in Sirius Black and in the young Tom Riddle, but the purest example in the Harry Potter book is undoubtedly the unfortunate Gilderoy Lockhart. The Ethical life (the position of many in the Ministry of Magic) develops out of a developing awareness of the limits and barrenness of the Aesthetic life, but it bases its relationship to God on following the rational rules of Hegelian/Kantian ethics, which it considers identical to Christian morality.

Neither of these is truly a religious life for Kierkegaard. Even the Ethical assumes that God makes no claim on humans that humans could not make on themselves by using their reason, so it has no need for revelation or for Christ. Kierkegaard points out that, if the Ethical were truly the Religious, Abraham's sacrifice of Isaac, rather than being the act that made him the Father of the faith, would be the worst sort of sin. Kierkegaard retells Abraham's story, and others much like it, repeatedly to explore all the possible variations on the question of whether there is a religious realm beyond the Ethical. He finds, not one, but two.

II

Fear and Trembling, like many of Kierkegaard's writings, is not attributed to Kierkegaard himself, but was written under a pseudonym, Johannes di Silentio. And Johannes is quite clear both that there are stages beyond the Ethical, and that, while a fervent admirer of Abraham, who represents the second stage beyond the Ethical, he has himself only attained the first. I argue in what follows that the understanding Johannes has attained, which some Kierkegaard scholars often refer to as Religiousness A is, in fact, a profound form of ontological humility. Further, I will use the distinction Kierkegaard himself makes between Religiousness A and Religiousness B to argue that the former is not in fact a form of religiousness at all, despite the powerfully Christian context of Kierkegaard's work, but an insight into how to live one's life that is independent of any specific belief system and, indeed, of any religious belief at all.

Johannes describes himself as a poet, and the "Eulogy on Abraham" in *Fear and Trembling* has several eloquently repetitive descriptions of the three paths through life, the penultimate description being, "There was one who relied on himself and gained everything; there was one who in the security of his own strength sacrificed everything; but the one who believed in God was the greatest of all." But the next, and last, repetition has four elements:

> There was one was great by virtue of his power; and one who was great by virtue of his wisdom; and one who was great by virtue of his hope, and one who was great by the virtue of his love, but Abraham was the greatest of all, great by that power whose strength is powerlessness, great by that wisdom whose secret is foolishness, great by that hope whose form is madness, great by the love that is hatred to oneself. (FTR 16–17)

Independence and power are the mandates of the Aesthetic (think again of the great Romantics of power such as Napoleon and Lord Voldemort). Self-sacrifice and wisdom are the mandates of everyday ethics, something anyone can understand. (One thinks of Remus Lupin's ethical arguments to justify leaving his wife for the good of their unborn child, arguments Harry effectively refutes.[37]) Belief in God, however, can lead in two directions—either toward hope and resignation, or toward love and faith, and both of these last two are paths of paradox.

For Kierkegaard, there are two necessary crises on the road to faith. First, there is what is now called the existential crisis, when a person realizes that, despite the philosophies of Descartes, Hegel, and so forth, life is not necessarily rational, the gods/God are not necessarily good, and death is inevitable. This is what happens in the moment God asks Abraham to sacrifice Isaac. The resulting state of Angst, or existential anxiety, must then be either faced and incorporated into how one understands the world, or fled, by ignoring the insight and burying oneself back in the safe, reasonable world of the Ethical. To live one's Angst means to step beyond ordinary rationality and can appear to be a regression to the premoral Aesthetic. For instance, Socrates, who Kierkegaard suggests was a Knight of Infinite Resignation, is seen now as a great philosopher. In his own time, however, public opinion was divided on whether he was the heroic martyr Plato gives us, or the groveling hypocrite portrayed by Aristophanes in *The Clouds*.[38]

III

All of which is basic existentialism. But Kierkegaard makes two further steps. He first describes the life that embodies such Angst, not as the joyful freedom from the constraints of traditional Christian or Kantian morality that is used to characterize it in much of twentieth-century secular existentialism, but as resignation, the need to live from and for something we cannot understand, often at a terrible price. Since he follows Hegel in regarding the Universal as the realm of both the Ethical and language, for Kierkegaard both forms of Religiousness must remain silent, unable to explain themselves to those around them (just as for much of his story Harry Potter cannot explain himself, even to those who love him most). "As soon as I speak, I express the universal, and if I do not do so, no one can understand me" (FTR, 60). At the same time, living beyond the universal destroys our ability to enjoy the seemingly harmless self-satisfaction available to those led by ordinary morality. Beyond language, there is no way of knowing whether my actions are right or wrong, whether I am saved or damned. Beyond the Ethical, there is only the need to follow the path that has been laid down for us, and constant humility in the face of what cannot be rationally explained.

Kierkegaard also posits a further crisis beyond the Ethical, one that Harry Potter never faces. While hard to describe, the essence of this crisis is the awareness that, despite it all, one can be certain of God's love. This is Kierkegaard's famous "leap of faith," and it is what separates the Knight of Infinite Resignation from the true Knight of Faith, Johannes from Abraham: "the knight of faith is the only happy man, the heir to the finite, while the knight of resignation is a stranger and an alien" (FTR, 50). The knight of faith inherits, "gets back" the finite by his willingness to surrender both it and the infinite (for Abraham to give up both Isaac and his role as Father of the faith) to the demands of the transcendent. Even for Kierkegaard, this step is neither easy nor a matter of human will. Johannes truly desires to be a knight of faith, but lacks the courage and remains a "mere" knight of infinite resignation (FTR, 34). The tragic hero "comes to the end of the story," but the knight of faith goes beyond that "by virtue of the absurd" (FTR, 115), that is, by virtue of faith. This is why "no poet can find his way to Abraham" as he could to Socrates and the "lower" realm of Religiousness he presents for Kierkegaard (FTR 118).

By following in this way the line Kierkegaard draws between Knight of Infinite Resignation and the Knight of Faith, we can see more clearly how a commitment to ontological humility can be severed from any particular system of religious belief (the realm of Religiousness B) and even exist independently of any religious belief at all (as his accusers argued it did for Socrates). Ontological humility, in its purest form, may even be incompatible with religious faith. Kierkegaard's Christian faith, after all, forced him to consign Socrates and hundreds, if not thousands, of other important thinkers who did not share that belief to a secondary status. There is a certain arrogance in his faith in the correctness of his own views and (of necessity) no adequate explanation of the basis of his certitude. My argument, however, is not with Kierkegaard. He is my ally insofar as he believes that infinite resignation, or ontological humility, is not religious faith, but at best a necessary precursor to true Christian belief.

The End of It All

Nothingness lies coiled in the heart of being—like a worm.
—Jean-Paul Sartre, *Being and Nothingness*

What I've said here illustrates fairly well that, while the concept of humility not only can link the Harry Potter saga to philosophy in an unexpected way, it can make important distinctions between seemingly similar philosophical enterprises (e.g., between Heidegger and much of twentieth-century existentialism) and become a bridge between seemingly very different projects, such as Frye's and Heidegger's, as well as between ethics at the one extreme and ontology at the other. And it does so while maintaining the openness to ambiguity and constructive skepticism that Code sees as central to feminist philosophy. This is possible because humility is an attitude toward whatever one may take to transcend human knowledge, whether that is taken as a more narrowly religious transcendence, as in Kierkegaard, an epistemological one, as we will see in Kant, an ontological one as in Heidegger, or an ethical one (and these can easily be, and often are, confused).

It is not surprising, therefore, that the term "ontological humility" has a brief history in the philosophical literature. It appears in French Christian existentialist Gabriel Marcel's diaries for 1929–1933, later published as the first part of *Being and Having*. That his thinking at that time reflects a religious variant on my use of the term is clear throughout these diaries. The entry for February 28, 1929, for instance, says, "From the very beginning there must be a sense of stewardship: something has been entrusted to us, so that we are not only responsible towards ourselves, but towards an active and superior principle." The clear link between this stewardship and something that has "been given to me"[39] reflects the connections between Heidegger's work and Marcel's. It is in a September 1934, footnote to an earlier entry that the words *ontological humility* appear. Marcel uses the term to name an attitude that he would assign to "the place which most traditional philosophers since Spinoza have given to freedom" (BH 133). We will see that the references to seventeenth-century Dutch philosopher Baruch Spinoza and to freedom aren't arbitrary. Marcel, however, never further develops the concept of ontological humility or applies it broadly to the thinking of other philosophers, although the same basic thinking recurs in his work under related concepts explored in these diaries: having, mystery, and fidelity.

Over fifty years later, in *The Experience of Freedom*, contemporary French philosopher Jean-Luc Nancy connects both Spinoza and freedom to what he calls "ontological generosity."[40] This generosity can be considered the counterpart of ontological humility, for example, when he says that "thinking is nothing other than the being-delivered to this generosity" (EF 55), which he later describes as "*a surprising generosity of [B]eing*" (EF 120).[41] Nancy says that Spinoza "attributed freedom exclusively to a God who was not a foundation but pure existence" (EF 12), that is, Being in Heidegger's sense of the word. (A judgment somewhat at variance with the discussion of Spinoza in the next chapter.) Nancy then offers what might be a definition of ontological humility in terms of this relationship between freedom and Being:

> There is no other task for thought, on the subject of freedom, than that which consists in transforming its sense of a property held by a subject into the sense of a condition or space in which alone something like a "subject" can eventually come to be born (or to die) *to* freedom (was this not already in some sense the effort of Spinoza's thought on freedom?). (EF 91–92, his emphasis)

Ontological generosity gives us a space in which our existence as "subjects," and a correlative freedom, are possible, just as the source of magic in J. K. Rowling's book gives her characters the space in which they can be witches or wizards. In both cases, the response to such a gift can only be ontological humility.

Nancy's language here is highly abstract, but he is clearly aware that when applied to concrete conditions in the world, the call to humility in all its forms is at the same time always political. If ontological humility in the face of our freedom is a call to recognize our own limitations, it requires that we also recognize the freedom of others whom we must, as the beings that we are, acknowledge as our equals in every way and who therefore are equally free.[42] If we are called, as Marcel says, to "stewardship," our relationship to both the human and nonhuman worlds cannot be one of destruction and exploitation. But what does this mean in actual, everyday political terms?

Take the current global political conflict over modernity, which is most often wrongly cast as a confrontation between Islam and "the West." A central issue in this conflict is the secularization of society and the demystification of the world, that is, the denial of the divine (or any form of transcendence) that we already saw is one hallmark of modernity and which believers of many faiths see as a serious challenge to their basic values. A local variant on the same conflict is the growth in the popularity, and political power, of conservative religious groups in the United States. Another example of a political arena where ontological humility could be brought to bear lies in the realm of what was called "sexual politics" when Frye's article was written, since much of the sexism she describes still unfortunately structures our thinking and popular culture. And there is the politics of the environment that Heidegger indirectly refers to, the political debate around the relationship between the human and the nonhuman that shows up, for instance, with regard to the preservation of natural habitats, the killing of predators to maintain a large population of prey species for hunting, or global warming.

To deny that we can even potentially have total knowledge and total control of the natural and human worlds, to underscore the gendered and racialized meaning of the desire for such control, and to assert that it is both a moral and a philosophical error even to try to create or maintain such control is to situate oneself clearly on one side or the other of these and many similar contemporary political issues. This is why ontological humility is more than just another way to sort thinkers or a footnote to Heidegger. The philosophical and political implications of humility as a basic orientation toward whatever transcends the human (which can be found even in such a canonical Anglo-American thinker as Hume) move its value beyond a "bridging" between traditions. A deeper understanding of this concept may prove to be more useful than "Continental" philosophy per se to anyone who would, as Code recommends, "assume responsibility for ourselves, for one another, and for the world" (AL 228).

Chapter One

Epistemological Humility and Its Other

Descartes

> The happiness [the Utilitarians] meant was not a life of rapture, but moments of such, in an existence made up of few and transitory pains, many and various pleasures . . . and having as the foundation of the whole not to expect more from life that it is capable of bestowing.
>
> —John Stuart Mill, *Utilitarianism*

I

"Epistemology" is the study of different theories of knowledge, of how we know things and how we can know when we know them. The philosophy of science, for instance, is a kind of epistemology that studies knowledge claims in the sciences. Epistemological humility would then be humility about the nature, extent, and reliability of human knowledge. The intrinsic link between that kind of humility and ontological humility should be clear: to think we can have absolute knowledge, even absolute knowledge that no knowledge is possible, is to deny human limitation, at least as regards our knowledge of the world. Conversely, epistemological humility, taken seriously enough, can become the grounds for ontological humility where it might not otherwise have developed, especially in philosophers who were not necessarily humble as human beings. One of the main lessons Harry Potter learns in the final book of the saga, as we have seen, is that he must surrender his "need to be sure, to know *everything*."[1]

Much of "modern" philosophy (philosophy roughly between 1600 and 1800) focuses mainly, although certainly not exclusively, on the need "to know *everything*," at least in part in response to the major scientific advances that were made during that time. The philosophers we will look at in this chapter represent three different major schools of thought about the nature and sources of human knowledge. This look backward to these three epistemological approaches will provide the historical context for the debates about knowledge, ontology, and humility in the twentieth century. At the same time, it will also offer some interesting examples of how different philosophical views can lead to a similar degree of humility and how similar philosophical views can lead to different attitudes toward what is implied in those philosophies about that which transcends human existence.

The epistemological focus of modern philosophy has its deepest roots in the work of René Descartes. He begins his "Discourse on Method" (1637) with what might appear to be appropriate epistemological humility: ". . . the power of forming a good judgment and of distinguishing the true and the false, which is properly speaking what is called Good Sense or Reason, is by nature equal in all men" (PWD-I 81). The impact of his words is weakened, however, when one learns that this sentiment was a common one in seventeenth-century philosophical writings. Thomas Hobbes, for instance, writes in *Leviathan* (1668) that "Nature hath made men so equal in the faculties of body and mind as that . . . when all is reckoned together the difference between man and man is not so considerable as that one man can thereupon claim to himself any benefit to which another may not pretend as well as he."[2] More doubt is cast on the epistemological humility of either Descartes or Hobbes when they go toe-to-toe in the acrimonious and unproductive debate in the "Objections and Replies" to Descartes's "Meditations" (PWD-II 60–78).

Similarly, Descartes's seeming epistemological humility ("the nature of man, in as much as it is composed of mind and body, cannot be otherwise than sometimes a source of deception" [PWD-I 198]) takes on a different tone when examined more closely. In proving God's existence in the Third Meditation, he says of his parents that,

> although all I have ever been able to believe of them were true, that does not make it follow that it is they who . . . [are] the authors of my being in any sense, in so far as I am a thinking being; since what they did was merely to implant certain dispositions in that matter in which the self—i.e. the mind, which alone I at present identify with myself—is by me deemed to exist.

He goes on to say that "For from the sole fact that God created me it is most probable that in some way he has placed his image and similitude upon me, and that I perceive this similitude . . . by means of the same faculty by which I perceive myself" (PWD-I 170). Some argue that this means Descartes's existence as a mind or "self" is due directly to God—a far from humble claim.[3] Moreover, this passage implies not only that is he created in the image of God, but also that he knows God (already a strong epistemological claim) in the same way that he knows himself.

If we can conclude from the prologue that religious belief is not a necessary condition for ontological humility, because even Kierkegaard believes such humility can exist outside of faith, our first lesson here may be that religious belief is not a sufficient condition for ontological humility either, since it seems to coexist in Descartes with a fairly high level of epistemological (and thereby ontological) arrogance. We noted in the prologue, too, what could be considered another dimension of Descartes's lack of ontological humility: his abandonment of Aristotelian final causes in favor of measuring the existence of a thing exclusively in terms of human needs because our inability to know the "[inscrutable] ends of God" means such final causes have "no useful employment" in science.[4] Descartes asserts instead that once he has proven the existence of God, "I have the means of acquiring a *perfect* knowledge of an infinitude of things," including "those which pertain to corporeal nature in so far as it is the object of pure mathematics," so long as that knowledge does not depend on whether whatever it is knowledge about actually exists or not (PWD-I 185, my emphasis).

II

But what good is knowledge that has nothing to do with the actual existence of things? (One hears echoes of a common accusation against Descartes in Hagrid's complaint about the centaurs from the Forbidden Forest at Hogwarts who, he tells Harry, aren't "interested in anythin' closer'n the moon."[5]) Descartes represents, and epitomizes, one major epistemological school in modern philosophy, Rationalism. Rationalism is the view that all knowledge must come from reason alone and not from our perception of actually existing things, since all perceptions can be doubted as possible illusions, dreams, or worse. For instance, Descartes concludes the Second Meditation by saying that "even [physical] bodies are not properly speaking known by the senses . . . , but by the understanding only" (PWD-I 157). He argues for this by showing that every sensory quality we experience in a piece of beeswax (color, shape, smell, consistency, etc.) changes when it melts, yet we know that it remains the same piece of wax. Since we cannot know this by anything our senses tell us (because they tell us different things in the two situations), Descartes concludes that we can only know it through reason, which provides us with the concept of a single physical substance that underlies all the changes in sensory qualities of the wax. The general argument of the first two Meditations leads Descartes to the conclusion that sense experience can always be doubted and so cannot be the basis of the absolutely certain knowledge he is seeking.

This search for absolutely certain knowledge, for certainty not beyond a reasonable doubt but beyond any possible doubt, or at least the belief that such certainty can be obtained, is the mirror opposite of epistemological humility. Such certainty might be found in fields such as logic or mathematics because they are self-contained abstract systems. Descartes's greatest scientific achievement was, of course, the invention of analytic geometry, and his fellow Rationalist Baron von Leibniz developed calculus independently of Sir Isaac Newton. What these Rationalists then do is to apply the standards and the methods of their success in mathematics to the very different problem of how we know the physical world around us.

But how could science work on the Rationalists' principle? Descartes offers several examples in Part V of "Discourse on Method." In discussing the human circulatory system, for instance, he assumes that the heart cannot be a muscle, since it never rests, and also that it has two chambers, like the lungs, rather than the four we now know it to have. On these bases, he considers the heart to be a relatively passive organ, again like the lungs, that is driven by heating and cooling of the blood. In general, science in this period tends to start with theories about how things work, often borrowed from Aristotle or others of the ancient philosopher-scientists, and derive applications or experiments from those theories, as opposed to the modern understanding of science as working in the opposite direction to develop theories out of experimental observations.[6] Alchemists knew the properties of gold, for instance, and used various methods to attempt to discover how to create it out of baser metals, but when those experiments failed, they didn't question what they knew about gold, which was part of a long and rich tradition, but rather tried different ways of achieving the same end. Despite their contributions to our knowledge of the chemical and physical world, they failed to question what they knew and how they had come to know it, that is, they lacked epistemological humility.

By taking the certainty and methods of mathematics as the basis for their epistemology, the Rationalists severed our knowledge of the world from that world itself because they underemphasized, or denied, the role of sense experience in how we know things. That some of them made great scientific advances in this way easily obscured the basic lack of ontological humility they showed in assuming that absolute certainty was not only the goal of human knowing, but was also obtainable by human minds. Even Spinoza, a Rationalist who, as a person, has the reputation of being one of the kindest and most humble of philosophers, wavers between the very strong epistemological claim, on the one hand, that he knows the nature of God and, on the other hand, the ontological humility to acknowledge that this knowledge reveals that God has an infinite number of attributes about which humans can have no knowledge at all.

There is no such ambivalence in Descartes. His philosophical stance is entirely compatible with the personality one might expect of a man who was fully aware that he had made one of the greatest mathematical advances in roughly two thousand years. While it is true that he does say things such as "we must confess that the life of man is very frequently subject to error in respect to individual objects, and we must in the end acknowledge the infirmity of our nature," note the limitation of this humility to "individual objects," that is, the everyday things around us, as opposed to the broader metaphysical truths he believes he has proven with absolute certainty. Moreover, he limits such humility to "the exigencies of action [that] often oblige us to make up our minds before having the leisure to examine matters carefully" (PWD-I199). In mathematics, science and philosophy, by contrast, where such exigencies don't exist, he implies that we can examine matters carefully enough to avoid any possible error. His limited humility here is a matter of practical limitations, not the inescapable humility in principle found in Spinoza.

III

In order to carry out the comparisons that are central to this chapter, we must focus on the three main metaphysical certainties Descartes believes his "method" can establish without any doubt. Up until now, however, the word "metaphysics" has only appeared here as something analytic philosophers were against. Since ontology is technically a species of metaphysics, a positive definition of metaphysics would seem to be required. Briefly, metaphysics can be understood as what must be known before one can do physics or any other kind of science, or as what is beyond (*meta-*) nature (*physis*): it is the study of the ultimate nature of reality and so also the study of what transcends reality. The three classic subdivisions of metaphysics—ontology, psychology, and theology—correspond to three core elements of Descartes's philosophy. This is not an accident, but rather one sign of Descartes's lack of ontological humility. Despite his insistence that he rejects "as false *everything* to which I could imagine the least ground of doubt" (PWD-I 101, my emphasis), he recapitulates many of the fundamental structures of the Aristotelian thought he is otherwise eager to toss aside.

There are deeper reasons, however, why Descartes, who begins by doubting everything, ends up showing neither epistemological nor ontological humility. Consider what the claim to doubt everything really means. Descartes bases this doubt on the fact that what the senses tell us can be false because of various illusions or because we are dreaming, and even what reason tells us could be false if there were an all-powerful "Evil Demon" determined to deceive us. The only thing he finds that he cannot doubt in this way is his own existence, from which he rebuilds a world knowable by reason due to the goodness of God. But could a human being every truly doubt *everything*? Descartes's defenders might object, as Hume does, that his doubt is "methodological," not a real doubt at all. If that is so, what must he assume about his method that gives it precedence over all the knowledge, philosophical or otherwise, that had been accumulated in the tradition up to his time? And what must he assume about himself?

Moreover, Descartes draws conclusions on the basis of his doubt that are not only often similar to traditional philosophical tenets, but also constitute very strong metaphysical and epistemological claims. One of Descartes's first distinctions in the "Meditations" is between himself as a "thinking thing" and his body (PWD-I 153). This generates a dualistic ontology (that is, the belief that there are two and only two kinds of being) based on a strict division between minds and material bodies: "because, on the one side, I have a clear and distinct idea of myself inasmuch as I am only a thinking and unextended thing, and as, on the other, I possess a distinct idea of body, inasmuch as it is only an extended and unthinking thing, it is certain that this I is entirely and absolutely distinct from my body and can exist without it" (PWD-I 190).

Genevieve Lloyd and many others have commented on the specific forms of the oppression of women that arise from such a sharp divide between the mind (always identified with men) and the body (subordinate to the mind and always identified with women).[7] It is also noteworthy that J. K. Rowling often invokes the distinction between mind (or soul) and body in the Harry Potter books, but she also has a concept of the mind that is at least partially material—think of the gray gas/liquid that reveals people's memories in Dumbledore's Pensieve.

Descartes's dualist ontology results in the sharply dualistic epistemology described above. Our knowledge of material bodies is subject to doubt insofar as it comes to us through the senses, which might deceive us. On the other hand, our knowledge of material things insofar as they exist in three-dimensional space, that is, insofar as they are the objects of mathematical and geometrical knowledge, has "some measure of certainty and an element of the indubitable" since these ways of knowing are purely rational and cannot, in the ordinary order of things, be doubted (PWD-I 147). With regard to human reason itself, moreover, our knowledge can be absolute: "I see clearly that there is nothing which is easier for me to know than my mind" (PWD-I 157).

Much of Descartes's theology is likewise allied with very strong metaphysical claim that becomes a key issue in modern philosophy, the nature of causal necessity. Aristotle tells us that it is necessary for everything that happens to have a cause, and necessary for the effect to occur once the causal event happens. Despite his claim to doubt everything, Descartes accept this traditional understanding of causality without question, including some of the less obviously true corollaries to it found in Scholasticism. In proving the existence of God in the Third Meditation, for instance, he posits without further argument, "that there must at least be as much reality in the efficient and total cause as in its effect" (PWD-I 162). He uses this premise to prove that, if he has the idea of an infinite substance, that is, God, then that idea must be caused by an infinite substance, and therefore God must exist.

He uses a similar causal principle in the argument referred to earlier in which he establishes that whatever caused his own existence must have "every perfection of which [he possessed] any idea," and would thus be God (PWD-I 168). Together these two arguments not only prove God's existence, but establish the divine nature as infinite and perfect, and, hence, incapable of the kind of deception that earlier, in the form of the "Evil Demon," made Descartes doubt that he was capable of knowing anything at all. After his meditations, by contrast, he is in a position to assure the Sacred Faculty of Theology at the Sorbonne that the proofs in the Meditations "are such that I do not think that there is any way open to the human mind by which it can ever succeed in discovering better" (PWD-I 135).

Does Descartes's lack of ontological humility make any difference in the contemporary world? His role in the last 400 years or so of world history could be understood as similar to the role Salazar Slytherin played in the rise of Lord Voldemort, his last heir, as recounted in *Harry Potter and the Chamber of Secrets*. Slytherin made the Dark Lord's work easier by championing "pure blood" witches and wizards against the "half-bloods" and "mudbloods"; he also created the Chamber of Secrets and apparently left in it the basilisk that nearly destroyed Harry. Similarly, Descartes created a philosophical mindset focused on certainty and ignored the pitfalls it created for his followers, arguably including

Spinoza, on the path to ontological humility. We already saw, in the discussion of Frye's article, Descartes's contribution to the creation of "the arrogant eye." Another way we can see how his views make a difference is the way they sets up terms and conditions of the philosophical conversation over the next 200 years that we will discuss in the rest of this chapter. A third way is the precedence of epistemology in later philosophy, precedence not only over what might be considered the more basic questions raised in metaphysics, but also over ethical and political concerns. Yet another way is the very starkness of the doubt with which he begins, which encourages skepticism, and defenses against it, as a primary philosophical preoccupation.

Finally, Descartes is in some ways indirectly responsible for the attitude that many people these days have about philosophy. Ask most older people who took a philosophy course while they were in college what they remember most about the course. Most likely, their response will be something along the lines of "The professor tried to convince the class that the table wasn't there." This probably isn't exactly what the professor said. Their instructor was more likely trying to re-create Descartes's doubt, which would lead to the conclusion that the students couldn't be *certain* the table was there. What people remember about the course, and about philosophy in general, however, is that it is nothing more than a mind game meant to confuse nonphilosophers, so that the professor (and ultimately Descartes) could look smart.

Hume

> When we run over libraries, persuaded by these principles, what havoc must we make? If we take in our hand any volume; of divinity or school metaphysics, for instance; let us ask, *Does it contain any abstract reasoning concerning quantity or number?* No. *Does it contain any experimental reasoning concerning matter of fact and existence?* No. Commit it then to the flames: For it can contain nothing but sophistry and illusion.
>
> —David Hume, *An Enquiry Concerning Human Understanding*

I

Where Descartes begins with doubt and moves to certain knowledge, David Hume can be said to begin with a certain kind of knowledge and move toward increasing doubt. He begins *A Treatise of Human Nature* (1739) with the unequivocal statement that "All perceptions of the human mind resolve themselves into two distinct kinds, which I shall call Impressions and Ideas."[8] By the end of *An Enquiry Concerning Human Understanding* (1748), he has reached the epistemological humility to speak of human beings "who must act and reason and believe; though they are not able, by their most diligent enquiry, to satisfy themselves concerning the foundation of these operations . . ." (ECHU 111). His ontological humility is even clearer in "Of the Immortality of the Soul" (published posthumously in 1777):

> Nothing in the world is perpetual. Every thing, however seemingly firm, is in continual flux and change: The world itself gives symptoms of frailty and dissolution: How contrary to analogy, therefore, to imagine, that one single form . . . is immortal and indissoluble? What a daring theory in that! How lightly, not to say how rashly, entertained![9]

Indeed, one could argue that no one in the European philosophical tradition has a keener sense of the limits of human knowledge than David Hume.

He achieves this by pushing the epistemological position opposed to Rationalism, Empiricism to its logical, if radical, conclusion. The first quotation above clearly describes the basic tenet of Empiricism, that our mental contents consist only of the "impressions" made on our senses when we perceive the world and the "ideas" that we form based on those impressions (although the exact terms used may vary among different Empiricist philosophers). One of Hobbes's complaints in his objections to Descartes's "Meditations," for instance, is directed against the contrary claim made by the Rationalists that our knowledge is based on reason alone: "But what shall we now say, if reasoning chance to be nothing more than the uniting and stringing together of names or designations by the word is?" Hobbes asks (PWD-II65). That is, many Empiricists would argue against Rationalism that logic, reason, might depend on, and reflect, our language, rather than the nature of reality. Interestingly, one trait that marks the Harry Potter saga as a thoroughly British story is the consistent and diligent Empiricism that seems to be the hallmark of a Hogwarts education. Lessons in magic are shown as exercises in experimental method, for instance, and everyone (including Rowling) takes a somewhat condescending attitude toward Professor Trelawney's purely abstract, generally useless, and most often illusory gift of prophecy.

The Empiricists were especially concerned to deny the possibility of the "innate ideas" of God, causality and the Self on which Descartes built his Rationalism. Although the most thorough refutation of innate ideas appears in the first book of John Locke's *Essay Concerning Human Understanding*[10] (1704), Hobbes had already challenged Descartes as to "whether the minds of those who are in a profound and dreamless sleep yet think. If not, they have at that time no ideas. Whence no idea is innate, for what is innate is always present." To this Descartes replied, "when I say that an idea is innate in us, I do not mean that it is always present to us. This would make no idea innate. I mean merely that we possess the faculty of summoning up the idea" (PWD-II 72–73), but he doesn't explain how we can know we have these innate ideas before we summon them in order to do so.

The seeds of Hume's theological humility, as we will see, are also laid by Hobbes's version of Empiricism when he objects, against Descartes, that "we have no image, no idea corresponding to [the most holy name of God] . . . Hence it appears that we have no idea of God," although in Hobbes's case he goes on to offer a brief version of his own causal proof of God's existence in the same paragraph (PWD-II 67). The Empiricist commitment to basing knowledge only on sense perception leads even Hobbes, whom his King referred to as "the great bear," to the edge (at least) of a form of ontological humility. Hume's more radical question is whether Empiricism can provide the basis for any knowledge at all, or whether it collapses into a skepticism that, as Hume says of the arguments of George Berkeley, "*admit of no answer and produce no conviction*" (ECHU, 107 fn).

II

Primary among Hume's arguments is the denial that we can have knowledge based on causal necessity. While he acknowledges that we have strong, even compelling, causal beliefs, Hume believes that they are based on nothing more than a habitual way of thinking that grows out of the constant conjunction of two successive events in our experience, leading us to expect the second event to follow whenever the first event occurs (ECHU 25–37). Therefore, causality cannot provide the grounds for philosophical arguments, most notably for Descartes's (and Hobbes's) proofs of the existence of God. Hume's basic argument about causality appears in essentially the same form both in the *Treatise* and the *Enquiry*, but here we will follow the version found in the latter work.

There Hume starts with the question of how we come to know anything that is not part of our present sensory experience or our memory of past experience. The answer is that we claim to know things about the world outside our experience through cause and effect reasoning.

Such reasoning, however, is not logical in nature, because the negation of a true causal claim is not logically impossible, but merely false. Logically, the sun *could* fail to rise tomorrow, although it won't. In addition, one can never infer what will occur in the future solely from perceiving the present causal conditions, the way one can follow a logical chain of implications. So, Hume concludes, our reliance on causal reasoning must be based on experience. That experience, however, is limited to our past and present sense experience. On what basis can we use causal reasoning to make inferences about events outside our experience? Only by using cause and effect reasoning, which is why this argument is often called "Hume's circle" (ECHU 15–25).

By reducing our reliance on causal reasoning to something analogous to the process whereby "animals, as well as men learn many things from experience, and infer, that the same events will always follow from the same causes" (ECHU 70), Hume both undermines Descartes's proofs that God exists and expresses a profound epistemological humility, even if in an arguably arrogant tone. He goes on to argue that, not only is causal belief not a result of reasoning in either humans or animals, but that it is "nothing but a species of instinct or mechanical power, that acts in us unknown to ourselves; and in its chief operations, is not directed by any such relations or comparisons of ideas, as are the proper objects of our intellectual faculties." Over a hundred years before Darwin, Hume put human "experimental" reasoning on a par with the instincts that teach birds how to sing (ECHU 72).

He goes further, however, by undermining even the starting point for Descartes's proof, the claim cited above that Descartes knows himself, with absolutely certainty, to be only a knowing thing or mind. Hume is more indirect about this claim in the *Enquiry*, but quite explicit in the appendix to the *Treatise*: "When I turn my reflexion on *myself*, I never can perceive this *self* without some [*sic*] one or more perceptions; nor can I ever perceive any thing but the perceptions. 'Tis the composition of these [perceptions], therefore, which forms the self" (THN 634, his emphasis). One might say that for Hume the mind is like a camera—it can create pictures (ideas) of other things, but can never take a picture of (or know) itself except as it might be reflected in a mirror, in which case the picture is not of it, but of its reflection. If the self, the mind, is only a composite of our perceptions and thoughts, it offers no basis for certain knowledge or for our concept of God.

By denying the possibility of innate ideas with the other Empiricists, and undermining the Cartesian concepts of Self, Causality, and God, Hume seems to leave us right where Descartes purports to begin. A claim to know that nothing can be known, however, is still a claim of absolute knowledge. Part of Hume's humility is his refusal to make that claim. He dismisses extreme, or "Phyrrhonian" skepticism because "all human life must perish, were [these] principles universally and steadily to prevail." He recommends instead a "mitigated" skepticism that would limit "our enquiries to such subjects as are best adapted to the narrow capacity of human understanding" and confine itself to "common life, and to such subjects as fall under daily practice and experience, leaving the more sublime topics to the embellishments of poets and orators, or to the arts of priests and politicians" (ECHU 110–112). This is why Hume concludes the *Essay* with the sweeping statement quoted at the beginning of this section—no claim to knowledge outside the realms of human experience and abstract reasoning, including Descartes's concepts of causality, God and a substantial Self, can be justified by merely human reason. One might as well, he implies, believe in miracles—or magic.

III

Hume's ontological humility, however, can be found in more than his epistemological claims. It is equally evident in his often-ignored work on morality and in his more noted work on rational theology in the posthumous "Dialogues Concerning Natural Religion." While Descartes, as already noted, tried to avoid moral questions, the other Rationalists, including Spinoza, joined Hume in offering a complete account of human psychology and morality as part of their work.[11] Hume's interest in, and unique approach to, moral issues is evident even in the *Essay*, which focuses primarily on epistemological questions. There he offers as an example of something that can be known directly through the definition of the terms it contains the claim that "where there is no property, there can be no injustice" (ECHU 113). This is because, for Hume, the state, and hence law and justice, were established to protect property. It is in the *Treatise*, however, and *An Enquiry Concerning the Principles of Morals* (1751), that his ethical views are fully developed, and his ontological humility most fully on display, albeit in a form that might seem, 200 years later, more equivocal than it does in the context of the mid-eighteenth century.[12]

He begins the third book of the *Treatise* by saying that "Morality is a subject that interests us above all others. . . . What affects us, we conclude can never be a chimera; and as our passion is engag'd on the one side or the other, we naturally think the question lies within human comprehension . . ."; then he adds an ironic, "Without this advantage I should never have adventur'd upon a third volume of such abstruse philosophy," although it is unclear how far that irony is meant to extend. His first question is the Empiricist one of how our judgments of right or wrong are related to sensory experience. Having already argued in the second book that reason cannot influence our emotions and, hence, our actions, he quickly concludes that "The rules of morality, therefore, are not conclusions of our reason" (THN 455–457). He also supports his claim by noting that, from an objective point of view, there is no difference between incest in humans and in animals, so the moral difference between the two cannot be a matter of experiential fact (THN 467–468). "Morality, therefore, is more properly felt than judg'd of . . ." (THN 470).

More specifically, according to Hume, actions we judge to be good are ones we associate with pleasure, actions we judge to be bad ones we associate with pain. Thus, Hume is a Utilitarian, but of a somewhat different stripe than John Stuart Mill.[13] Hume says that "We do not infer a character to be virtuous, because it pleases: But in feeling that it pleases after such a particular manner, we in effect feel that it is virtuous" (THN 471). There is a role for theory here, however, as noted above with regard to injustice. Justice is, for Hume, an "artificial" virtue in the sense that it arises out of "the circumstances and necessity of mankind," but he adds that, although the rules of justice may be "*artificial,* they are not *arbitrary*" (THN 477–478). Unlike Hobbes, who believed humans sacrificed a large part of their right of self-determination to their king in exchange for the protection of civil society, Hume believes it is only the right to claim or control the goods of others that our ancestors surrendered as the condition of living in peace with their neighbors, who would otherwise have been in constant competition with them for the limited material goods the world provides. As Hume said in the *Inquiry,* once property rights are established, "there immediately arise the ideas of justice and injustice" (THN 490).

What has happened to pleasure and pain here? As Hume explains, "*Thus self-interest is the original motive to the* establishment *of justice: but a* sympathy *with public interest is the source of the* moral approbation *which attends that virtue*" (THN 499–500). He then gives a detailed account of how this sympathy works, both in the case of justice and in other moral virtues. With regard to justice, the argument relies on the inherently social nature of human beings. "As much as we value our own happiness and welfare, [so] much must we applaud the practice of justice and humanity," he tell us, "by which alone the social confederacy can be maintained, and every man reap the fruits of mutual protection and assistance."[14] Justice promotes the social good, which promotes our happiness. In cases that don't directly affect us, we make judgments of approval or disapproval based on our ability to sympathize with those whose happiness is directly affected, which again makes it a matter of our own pleasure or pain: "wherever we go, whatever we reflect on or converse about, everything still presents us with the view of human happiness or misery, and excites in our breast a sympathetic movement of pleasure or uneasiness" (HE 221). This is the basis of all morality for Hume.

The important thing to note, however, is that he never takes the step that is central to Utilitarianism—Hume never says "pleasure is good." This is what makes him arguably a Knight of Infinite Resignation—he understand, as Harry Potter comes to, that we must make moral choices without any way to be certain of their goodness. Hume's is a purely descriptive form of Utilitarianism that attempts to stay firmly on the side of facts in the fact/value distinction that he helped to establish. Values, for him, are matters of emotion, whereas his enterprise is one of reason, or rather, one of exploring the limits of reason. Reason can only describe how the human mind and human passions work; it cannot tell us how we should act, merely on what principles we will decide which acts are good and evil. And the conclusion of this impassive reason is that "there never was any quality recommended by any one, as a virtue or moral excellence, but on account of its being *useful*, or *agreeable* to a man *himself*, or to *others*" (HE 336).

Hume's ontological humility, it is worth noting, brings out what might be called a "proto-feminist" aspect to his work. Annette Baier argues that he could be labeled both a "women's moral theorist"[15] and a "reflective women's epistemologist."[16] She doesn't cite anything like humility as the reason (perhaps because she seems to have a rather narrow sense of humility [HRWE 28]), but rather his outsider status as a member of a conquered nation writing in another nation's language that made him, "if you like, an unwilling virtual woman" (HRWE 22). Not that he favored the views of "bluestockings," although Baier cites the relatively liberal attitudes toward women reflected in his ideal commonwealth (HRWE 29) and some of his later essays (HRWE 35). Rather, as we saw earlier, there is an intrinsic link between the refusal of absolute knowledge and the search for absolute mastery, on the one hand, and ways of thinking that are culturally coded for us as "feminine," on the other. As Baier says, "Hume's epistemology . . . is like the moral epistemology he goes on to articulate, fallibilist and cooperative" (HRWE 31), much like the views put forward by Code, Frye, and other contemporary feminist philosophers.

In the last work Hume prepared for publication, "The Dialogues Concerning Natural Religions," he carries his epistemological humility, and perhaps his irony, to new heights. Heights so high, one commentator notes, that he can be credited with the nineteenth-century "fideism," or religious belief against all reason, that reached its own height in Kierkegaard (although probably without Hume's influence in that case).[17] Scholars even remain uncertain which of the three main characters in the "Dialogues" speaks for Hume himself. Most rule out Demea, the orthodox Christian whose views tend to remind the reader of Berkeley, but remain undecided between Philo, the skeptic who echoes much of what Hume says elsewhere, and Cleanthes, whom Pamphilus, the "recorder" of the "Dialogues," credits at the end of the dialogues with being "still nearer to the truth" (DCNR 89).

Cleanthes offers a proof of the existence of God that was common among intellectuals in the seventeenth and eighteenth centuries. He describes the world as a great machine, then says, "Since therefore the effects resemble each other, we are led to infer, by all the rules of analogy, that the causes also resemble, and that the Author of Nature is somewhat similar to the mind of man, though possessed of much larger faculties, proportioned to the grandeur of the work he has executed" (DCNR 15). Much of the rest of the "Dialogues" is spent attacking this argument, but Hume himself espoused this view earlier in a footnote to the appendix of the *Treatise*:[18] "The order of the universe proves an omnipotent mind." This could be taken as an attempt to lessen the skeptical impact of the earlier work, except that it is appended to the radical denial that I have any idea of "self." The footnote merely notes that, although this denial of a substantial self undermines any possibility we might have an idea of God, "this can have no effect on either religion or morals" because of the obvious truth of [the above] argument" (THN 633). Still, scholars remain divided on Hume's religious views, proving perhaps that his humility is so complete he even stays out of the spotlight in what he knew would be his final work.

Kant

> This deduction . . . was the most difficult task ever undertaken in the service of metaphysics . . .
>
> —Immanuel Kant, *Prolegomena to Any Future Metaphysics*

I

Immanuel Kant credits Hume with awakening him from his "dogmatic slumber"[19] and setting him on the course that made Kant one of the most influential philosophers in the modern period, second only to

Descartes. Kant's project was to rescue philosophy from Hume's skepticism and to synthesize Rationalism and Empiricism into a single system that respects the role of perception and reason alike. Some might consider him to be a thinker like Spinoza, one whose ultimate position of humility was based on the assumption that he could, and did, have certain knowledge about the nature of reality. Certainly the quotation above has the tone of someone closer to Gilderoy Lockhart than to Dumbledore. Kant's philosophy, however, does not require knowledge of the nature of either God or reality, but rests on a respect for the limits of human knowledge that, I would argue, almost approaches Hume's. This is because Kant focuses, not on what we can or do know, but on the form our knowledge must take.

The "must," of course, suggests that Kant's position is also more complex than Hume's, since it allows for a necessity that is not strictly logical. As we've seen, Hume divides our knowledge into empirical claims and logical ones. His concept of logic depends on the concept of analytic truth, that is, truth based on the definitions of the terms involved, such as "All bachelors are unmarried men" and, on Hume's account, the claim that without private property there is no civil state, hence no justice, hence, also no injustice. For him, this is why causal claims aren't matters of "abstract reasoning" because the occurrence of an effect cannot be inferred from the occurrence of its cause and the relevant definitions alone. As we saw, he also notes that it is not a logical contradiction to say that a cause might fail to produce its usual effect. What motivated Kant was his conviction that this apparently unremarkable reliance on traditional logic was the fatal flaw that led to Hume's skepticism. More importantly, Kant thought he knew what was wrong with the traditional way of thinking.

Kant's basic argument is that mathematics and geometry are not analytic in the way Hume believes. Kant says we cannot deduce the geometrical truth that the shortest distance between two points is a straight line from the definitions of the terms involved (and some twentieth-century mathematicians would say it may not even be true). Similarly, he claims there is nothing in the definitions of the numbers 7, 5, and 12 and the words *plus* and *equals* that would led to the conclusion that $7 + 5 = 12$ without a further "intuition" of the number of points represented by 7 and 5. (The German word he uses, *Anschauung*, means literally a contemplation or perception, but not necessarily of an empirical object—it doesn't have the connotation the English "intuition" has of a nonrational way of knowing.) Kant believes mathematics is based on the pure intuition of time (think counting) and geometry on the pure intuition of space, where "pure" means empty of any specific content, an intuition merely directed at moments in time or lines in space. This experience remains "a priori," or independent of our experience. Even if our experience were radically different than it is—magical, for instance—it would still occur in time and space. But the knowledge pure intuitions yield is also "synthetic," as opposed to analytic, because that knowledge was not already present in the definitions of the terms (PAFM 14–16).

The possibility of "a priori synthetic" knowledge is what ultimately allows Kant to "remove Hume's doubt" (PAFM 53), but it is also the weakest link in his argument because it is always possible simply to deny that such a thing as a priori synthetic knowledge exists. This is the source of the contemporary split between "Continental" and "Anglo-American philosophy" discussed in the Prologue. "Continental" philosophers consider Hume's skepticism to be a *reduction ad absurdum* argument against Empiricism because they believe his arguments prove that no knowledge at all can be based purely on our sensory experience. Since they share the Empiricists' rejection of innate ideas, they see the priori synthetic as the only possible way to ground knowledge. Even those "Continental" philosophers who might reject a foundationalist project retain the belief that all philosophy before Kant is what they call "precritical" and, therefore, seriously flawed. English language philosophers, on the other hand, generally reject Kant's arguments with regard to a priori synthetic knowledge and do philosophy largely within the confines of Hume's "mitigated skepticism," which is why it remains primarily "analytical." This philosophical position does raise perplexing questions about the nature of mathematical and geometrical truths, but philosophers in that tradition solve them by asserting that they are, in fact, analytic or arguing that they are high-level empirical generalizations. They consider these positions easier to defend than Kant's claim to have found an entirely new kind of knowledge.

II

While mathematics and geometry prove the existence of a priori synthetic knowledge for Kant, its real importance is in metaphysics. He claims to have replicated Hume's argument about causality with other metaphysical concepts and concludes that "metaphysics consists altogether" of a priori synthetic concepts (PAFM 6). The question then is, What are the objects of the intuitions underlying metaphysical concepts that correspond to time and space in mathematics and geometry? Those objects, Kant tells us, are the empty forms of the judgments we make about sensory objects: "judgments of experience take their objective validity, not from the immediate cognition of the object (which is [as the Rationalists said] impossible), but merely from the conditions of the universal validity of empirical judgments . . ." (PAFM 42). Perception will never give us the concept of a material substance that persists through every change in the sensory qualities of Descartes's piece of wax. Since the Empiricists have proven the impossibility of an innate idea of such a substance, Kant's solution is that *"the understanding does not derive its laws (a priori) from, but prescribes them to, nature"* (PAFM 62). That is, we don't perceive substance, but must assume it exists in order to make sense out of our perceptual experience. (Similarly, Harry Potter never considers the possibility of something like his friend Hermione's Time-Turner, even when he sees her effectively in two places at once, because the Time-Turner's ability to move her backward in time and live through the same hour twice violates the way time forms our experience.[20])

Thus, concepts such as causality and substance, like time and space, are not part of the world as it exists in itself, but part of how we perceive the world, ways in which we must organize perceptions so they can serve as a basis for our interaction with the physical world. At least since Descartes, philosophers had recognized that some properties of sensory objects (those Locke called "secondary qualities," such as color, smell, taste, and sound) clearly vary between perceivers of the same object at the same time, and between a single person's perception of the same object at different times (e.g., under different light conditions). They were called secondary because Locke assumed that they were caused by the interaction of the primary qualities of objects (today's equivalent would be their molecular properties) and human sense organs. Later, Berkeley argued that it was impossible to determine which sensory qualities are primary and which secondary in this sense. Kant pushes this argument a step further by saying everything we know about an object is a result of interaction between the "thing-in-itself" and the human mind. He differentiates his view from Berkeley's "mystical and visionary idealism" because he doesn't deny the existence of things-in-themselves outside of experience (PAFM 37).

According to Kant, when we encounter an object there occurs something like an instantaneous process that can be broken down into two discrete sets of questions that we in effect ask about it in order to situate it in reality as we know it. The first set contains the questions that place the object in time and space: Where is it? and When is it? These "forms of the intuition" (time/number and space) are, as we have seen, the basis of geometry and mathematics. The second set of questions move the perception beyond intuition to understanding, or everyday public knowledge. They ask of the object such questions as Where does it fit in the causal chain of empirical reality? Is its existence necessary or just a matter of fact? Is it a single thing or many? and Is it really there? Once we have answers to these questions and the others in this set (there are twelve categories of the understanding in all), we can be said to know the object completely insofar as it is part of our experienced world (PAFM 46). This makes science possible. Since the behavior of human beings is part of our experienced world, it also makes the social sciences possible, and they owe their existence in the form we know them today largely to Kant.

What this doesn't make possible is any knowledge of things, whether material objects or human minds, as they are in themselves. This is where Kant avoids Spinoza's arrogance (although in every way as human beings he was reportedly the more arrogant of the two). Everything Kant has said about our knowledge of the experienced world, he points out, is validated by our everyday knowledge of objects, along with the a priori synthetic sciences of mathematics, and geometry. Reality makes rational sense to us. Hume has proven that it shouldn't, if matters of fact and abstract reasoning are our only sources of knowledge. Therefore, there must something else that grounds our understanding of the world, that is, there must be a priori synthetic knowledge based on the pure forms of our experience of sensory objects. Our knowledge, however, stops there for Kant. His four antinomies, or apparent paradoxes, show that there is no one answer to traditional metaphysical questions about the ultimate nature of the experienced world (Is the world limited or unlimited? Is it simple or composite? Do we have free will? Is there a God?) because our reality is not self-sufficient, but depends on the existence of unknowable things-in-selves, including our own minds (PAFM 80). Human knowledge is, at best, limited and partial. This is what contemporary philosopher Rae Langton has called "Kant's humility."[21]

Kant bases his metaphysical and epistemological humility on a powerfully dualistic ontology, but one very different from Descartes's. In place of Descartes's division of reality into minds and bodies, Kant divides both minds and bodies in two, giving each of them an existence as part of human reality and an existence independent of our experience. He draws a sharp line between the experienced world and what he calls the "intellectual world," where those things we must assume exist but cannot experience have their being. These include the material things-in-themselves that cause our perceptions; our own substantial selves insofar as they are the source (as opposed to the object) of our conscious experience and, by extension, the concept of substance per se; causal necessity and, by extension, the idea of the natural world as a unified causal system with God as its source. These three Ideas of pure reason are not objects of our knowledge, but its limiting conditions. Even the idea of God remains an empty one. Kant concludes, "We must therefore think an immaterial [realms of things in themselves], a world of understanding, and a Supreme Being, . . . because in them only, as things in themselves, reason finds . . . completion and satisfaction . . ." (PAFM 95). For Kant, the ultimate knowledge can only be of the limits of what we can know.

DESCARTES

Mind	Body
perfectly known	imperfectly known through the senses, except insofar as known through math and geometry

KANT

Intelligible World	Experienced World
mind and body [and God] in themselves and so not known	mind and body known in terms of time/space and the categories(substance, cause)

III

A further advance that Kant claims to have made over Hume is the ability, based on his sparse ontology, to derive an absolute basis for moral judgment. The fact/value distinction, the sharp divide between what we can know from sensory experience and abstract ideas, and the passions that guide our actions, follows from the Hume's Empiricist assumptions about both knowledge and the emotions. Nothing in bare perception gives us moral qualities, and reason cannot move us, Hume tell us, so the only possible moral theory is a descriptive Utilitarian one. By introducing the possibility of a priori synthetic knowledge, however, Kant opens up the possibility of a logic that could speak, if not to our empirical selves, perhaps to our wills as entities in the intelligible world. This, in turns, opens the possibility of a universal, absolute ethical system free of any religious basis.

For Hume, since causes and effects are as closely tied together in human behavior as they are in the material world, the necessity we attribute to physical causation is present in human actions as well (THN 405). This means there is no free will, and our sense of having a choice as to how we act is an illusion. For Kant, causality has its place only in the experienced world, so our wills, not existing in that world, can be free. Moreover, since we experience ourselves as making free choices, we are "free from a practical point of view."²² But what kind of law can determine a free will? Kant finds the answer in an empty formula analogous to the empty forms that are the basis for other a priori synthetic knowledge. The only law a good will can obey is the law that it should obey the law: "I should never act except in such a way that I can also will that my maxim should become a universal law" (GMM 14). More concretely, Kant's "categorical imperative" can be restated as "Act in such a way that you treat humanity, whether in your own person in the person of another, always at the same time as an end and never simply as a means," because we each regard our own rationality as an end-in-itself, and, since no justifiable distinction can be made between one rational being and another, we must extend this respect to the rationality of others (GMM 36).

Despite Kant's undisputed place in the pantheon of political liberalism, however, this last detail may be the one where the devil lurks. Who, after all, is to be considered a "rational being"? In Harry Potter's world there are a number of creatures who use language and even have rudimentary culture, such as the garden gnomes and giants, whose stupidity seems to make their status as full members of society doubtful even for the heroes of Rowling's saga. In Kant's time, that was the general opinion of women and people of color (still defined then literally by the color of their skin). If one hallmark of rationality for Kant is moral autonomy, the ability to act freely according to the categorical imperative, then those whose capacity for free action is subject to severe cultural or economic constraints remain, as women do for Kant, not fully rational beings. Baier notes that in his ideal commonwealth, in contrast to Hume's, "women and servants have to rely on propertied men to look after their interests (indeed to say what those interests are)" (HRWE 30). While his ontological humility requires Kant to create a space in which all humans could be considered rational and equal, as a matter of historical fact, for him some rational beings are more equal than others.

But isn't Kant's categorical imperative a claim to certain moral knowledge? In at least three important ways, it isn't. On the practical level, it remains an empty moral rule Kant seldom fills out with examples (GMM 10–12). He is, like Hume, clearly not in the business of giving moral advice. On a metaphysical level, it would do no good for him to give advice in any case, because we can never fully know the reasons behind our actions: "We like to flatter ourselves with the false claim to a more noble motive; but in fact we can never, even by the strictest examination, completely plumb the depths of the secret incentives of our actions" (GMM 19). This is epistemological humility in the moral realm taken to a new high (or low). And finally, Kant recognizes that his ethical theory has a potentially fatal flaw:

> One must frankly admit that there is here a sort of circle from which, so it seems, there is no way to escape. In [the experienced world] we assume that we are free so that we may think of ourselves as subject to moral laws in the [intellectual realm]. And we then think of ourselves as subject to these laws because we have attributed to ourselves freedom of the will. (GMM 52)

For Kant, however, we truly do exist as caused, insofar as we exist in the experienced world, which can be understood only in terms of causal relations, and as free insofar as we exist in the intellectual world—the world of things-in-themselves, where causal relationship don't apply.[23]

Not a very satisfactory solution, of course, but one that links Kant's ethics and his ontology into a single system that became, with its variants, an incredibly powerful force in the world for the next 200 years. So why include Kant among the examples of ontological humility? The above should make it clear that, whatever his followers may have made of his philosophy, his sole concern was with the limits, not the content, of human knowledge and human moral reason. Where Hume might be accused of arrogance in his assertions of what we cannot know, Kant refutes him, not by claims to human knowledge, but by drawing its boundaries. Moreover, he draws those boundaries so as to exclude from the realm of the knowable the basic certainties Descartes left outside the scope of his doubt: self, causality, god, morality. Beyond that, Kant tells us that "the moral law inevitably humbles every man when he compares the sensuous propensity of his nature with the law."[24] Despite the humbling effect of his philosophy, Kant insists that "Two things fill the mind with ever new and increasing admiration and awe, the oftener and more steadily we reflect on them: the starry heavens above me and the moral law within me" (CPR 166).

Chapter Two

Ontological Humility in Heidegger

The Thrownness of Dasein

> The essence of art is poetry. The essence of poetry, in turn, is the founding of truth.
>
> —Martin Heidegger, "The Origin of the Work of Art"

I

It might be argued that one can only find the pattern of ontological and epistemological humility or arrogance in the authors discussed in the last chapter if one is looking for it (and, some might argue, not even then). But where does the idea that such a pattern exists come from? As suggested in the Prologue, the basic insight behind the concept of ontological humility can be found in the work of Martin Heidegger. In this chapter we will trace that claim through three areas of Heidegger's work: his unfinished opus *Being and Time* (1929) and other texts that are part of the so-called early Heidegger; his readings of ancient Greek philosophical texts over the full length of his career; and the critiques of technological modernity that are the best known and most accessible of his later writings. Despite the earlier/later Heidegger division, we will find he is occupied, if not preoccupied, with ontological humility from the beginning of his philosophical career. As early as a lecture course in 1921–1922, he declares, almost in the spirit of Hume, that "Skepticism . . . is the beginning of philosophy, and as the genuine beginning, it is also the end of philosophy."[1] Before moving into Heidegger's work in more detail, however, key terms need to be explained, and we need to remind ourselves that ontological humility often doesn't correspond to being a humble person.

To begin with the somewhat cryptic title of this section, "Dasein" (literally, in German, "to be there"[2]), is Heidegger's term for what the French existentialists call "human existence." As we shall see, Heidegger is deeply suspicious of the concept of "humanity" and how it has been understood in the philosophical tradition, so he uses the term Dasein to focus, not on humans as a biological species, but as beings who are aware that they exist in a specific time and place, that they are "there" when they could have been in some other place or time—or nowhere at all, since Dasein is also defined as a being who is aware of its own eventual death. His ontology consists, not of minds and bodies (and God), as in Descartes, or of experienced and intellectual worlds, as in Kant, but of beings (entities in the world that are not Dasein), Dasein, and Being, which is transcendent to both.

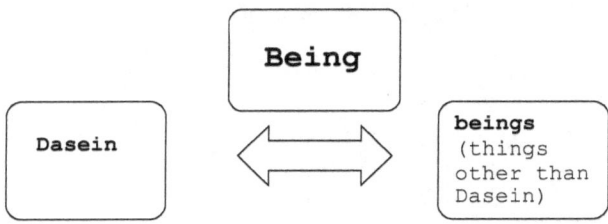

One way to understand the difference between the earlier and later Heidegger is as a shift from a focus on Dasein to a primary interest in Being itself.

"Thrownness" is how a specific instance of Dasein (the most correct way to describe an individual person for Heidegger) comes to be in the time and place where it finds itself, or more correctly, the bare fact that it finds itself there. What "throws" Harry Potter into his world as "the boy who lived" is Voldemort's murder of his parents and his attempt to kill Harry. This "thrownness" then determines everything that happens to him in Rowling's saga. The importance of time in *Being and Time* can be seen by understanding this thrownness as the past, beginning with our appearance/birth at a random spot in the world and consisting of everything that we have done or that has happened to us since that moment. Even after the death of the Dark Lord, time is measured for Harry at the end of *Harry Potter and the Deathly Hallows* by the absence of pain in the scar, which represents how his essential thrownness is marked. The last words in his story are "The scar had not pained Harry for nineteen years. All was well."[3]

For Heidegger, Dasein exists as "thrown projection," that is, our past, our thrownness, is important or meaningful only because of how we project ourselves into a completely open future.[4] Our projects, our goals, from the most trivial (don't forget to buy bread) to the most elevated (make the world a better place) are what give meaning to and define every aspect of our lives. More important, they are what makes us who we are. For Heidegger, as for Hume and Kant, human consciousness isn't a substantial Cartesian Self, but an empty directedness at whatever it is consciousness *of*. What we take to be our "Self" is an object of consciousness—the self known to us and to others through our actions, words, and so on, and known to us also through our thoughts when we reflect on them—not consciousness itself. Heidegger says that "In the structure of thrownness, as in that of projection, there lies essentially a nullity" (BT 331). Awareness of this nullity, or emptiness, at the core of our existence is the basis of the existential Angst we discussed earlier in relation to Kierkegaard.

One more thing needs to be said by way of introduction to Heidegger. Just as most people who have taken a college philosophy course remember the Cartesian table that wasn't there, referred to in the last chapter, most people who have heard of Heidegger will say, "But wasn't he a Nazi?" He was. He joined the Nazi party in 1933, when he became Rector of the University of Freiburg, where among his other duties he fired all Jewish faculty members, including his teacher, Edmund Husserl. It is not insignificant, however, that he resigned the Rectorship after only one year and that by 1938, when he first presented "The Age of the World Picture," he felt it necessary to suppress almost half of the paper, now published as an appendix (QT x). One could assume that by then he had realized what a monumental error he had made in signing on with the Nazi cause. One might also assume that such an experience would leave him a changed human being. In that case, one would probably be wrong. While Heidegger's thinking does undergo a major shift roughly between 1929 and 1935, there is also a strong continuity of thought on certain questions (including ontological humility), and he never made significant public comment on his association with National Socialism[5]—more proof that ontological humility, unfortunately, carries no necessary implications for how a person lives her or his life.

II

What is now published as *Being and Time* is, in fact, only Part One of what was projected as a two-part work, the second half of which was never written. It is itself broken into two "divisions," the first an analysis of Dasein, the second an interpretation of Dasein's relationship to time. Most scholars regard the second division as where Heidegger felt himself begin to go wrong, but echoes of the first still appear in papers, such as "The Origin of the Work of Art," that were written during the transitional period between the earlier and the later stages of his thought. Division One also provides the philosophical basis for much of the twentieth-century existentialism discussed in the next chapter. For these reasons, we will focus here on Division One and the ways in which it shapes, and is shaped by, the importance of ontological humility in Heidegger's work.

The very beginning of *Being and Time*, before the heading "Part One," sets it in the context of both epistemological humility and ontology: "Do we in our time have an answer to the question of what we really mean by the word 'being'? Not at all. . . . Our provisional aim is the Interpretation of *time* as the possible horizon for any understanding whatsoever of Being" (BT 19). A translator's footnote indicates that "horizon" in Heidegger is closer to "limit" than the usual sense of the English word so that, for Heidegger, as for Kant, the limiting condition of Dasein's understanding of Being is time.[6] Dasein is defined by the fact that "Being is an *issue* for it" (BT 32), which gives it an a priori ontological priority over beings that are not Dasein. Our most basic relationship to those other entities, however, is not simple perception, as in Descartes, Hume, or Kant, but our everyday involvement with the things around us.

According to Heidegger, objects present themselves to us most directly as equipment, as things such as hammers or pens or books that we use as we move through life and find "ready-to-hand." Occasionally, we find them as "unready-to-hand," that is, not there or not working as they should. When that happens, we might see them as "present-at-hand," as objects of perception completely outside the context of their use.[7] For Heidegger, seeing things primarily as the object of abstract perception (the way they are seen by Descartes, Hume, and Kant) is derivative and secondary.

Ready-to-hand	Hammer hammering	Not an explicit object of attention
Unready-to-hand	Broken hammer	Focus on how to fix it
Present-at-hand	Hammer as bare object (Descartes' piece of wax)	Disinterested focus on its properties

Equipment has two further characteristics. First, it must "withdraw in order to be ready-to-hand" (BT 99). That is, equipment is effectively invisible in use because the user's attention is focused on what the equipment is used for. The clearest example of this in our world would be a person's glasses, which are both literally and theoretically invisible when one looks *through* them to see something else. The clearest example in Harry Potter's world would be his wand, which is almost an extension of himself (remembering that "it's really the wand that chooses the wizard, of course"[8]). Normally we only notice equipment when it fails.

The second thing to remember about equipment is that is always imbedded in what Heidegger calls an "equipmental totality." This means it is an integral part of a complex set of things and practices that are needed to carry out the projects that define Dasein's life. Since equipmental totalities are public and shared, those projects also must exist as part of a larger social world. A long chapter of the first Harry Potter book is devoted to describing the social meaning of the magical items he counters on Diagon Alley (e.g., that toads as pets are out of style[9]). For this reason, Dasein's projects always refer to other Dasein and "a bare subject without a [social] world . . . is [never] given" (BT 152). Dasein's existence is always "being-with" the other Dasein who share the same social world. Most of the time, this being-with takes the form of submersion in the "They," living by the generally accepted social definitions of one's time, place, social class, and so on. "One" (the singular of the "they") graduates from college (or from Hogwarts), watches this or that television show, learns to drive a car, so these become projects for us insofar as we are part of the "they-self." This they-self provides us with the "referential context," within which our projects and, therefore, our lives can have meaning (BT 167).

The they-self, however, also obscures important aspects of our existence from us. Notably, it hides its own historical contingency and presents its world, real or magical, as both natural and necessary. This is where the existentialism outlined in the Prologue comes into play. In the moment of Angst an individual Dasein realizes both the lack of intrinsic meaning in its life and its complete freedom from the social meanings created by the they-self. Heidegger sees this release from social constraint as a source of anguish and an opportunity to redefine one's life in an "authentic" way. By "authentic" he means a life based, not on some essential Cartesian Self, but on the free choices of a Dasein who knows those choices to be arbitrary just because they are free. In this way, we can embody the existential truth that existence precedes essence, creating our Selves from what we choose to be, rather than acting out the roles dictated by society. For Heidegger, however, authenticity is possible only on the background of the meanings provided by the they-self—"*authentic* existence is not something which floats above . . . everydayness; existentially, it is only a modified way in which such everydayness is seized upon" (BT 224). Only on the background of the Danish Christendom he despised could Søren Kierkegaard encounter the Absolute.

III

Existentialism is not necessarily ontological humility. Notice, however, how far we have come from Descartes's certainty about causality, Self, and God, or even from Hume's certainty that truth can be found only in empirical propositions or analytic statements. We have encountered human existence as empty at its core, based largely on socially sanctioned fabrications about its true nature, and capable of escaping the they-self only in a partial and attenuated way. The depth of Heidegger's ontological humility becomes much clearer when seen in the contrast between his work and the existentialism of Jean-Paul Sartre in Heidegger's response to Sartre's "Existentialism is a Humanism." While this response, "Letter on Humanism," appeared well into the later period of Heidegger's thought, by focusing on those aspects of it that refer directly to the tenets in *Being and Time*, the most existentialist of his major works, we can see both the differences between his views and Sartre's, and the underlying continuity in Heidegger's thought with regard to ontological humility.

First of all, Heidegger denies that individual Dasein is the most "essential" form of human existence. Rather, for him the individual is merely the negation of the public they-self, in large part because "language comes under the dictatorship of the public realm, which decides in advance what is intelligible and what must be rejected as unintelligible" (BW 221). He rejects the term "humanism" because of its history as part of traditional metaphysics, which ignores Being in favor of beings, and also misunderstands Dasein itself as if it were merely another species of beings, "a rational animal" in Aristotle's terms (BW 227). For Heidegger, Sartre, like Nietzsche, makes the mistake of attempting to undo metaphysics by reversing the traditional values it embodies. Heidegger even rejects what we will see is the dictum of existentialism, "existence precedes essence," because "the reversal of a metaphysical statement remains a metaphysical statement" (BW 232). Metaphysics in any form, for Heidegger, is a claim to know what we do not, and possibly cannot, know (BT 42-44).

The thrownness of Dasein proves the "Man" of humanism is not what we should concern ourselves with, because the randomness of how we come to exist where and when we do is just a symptom of the broader fact that "Man does not decide whether and how beings appear . . ." (BW 234). (It is noteworthy that German allows Heidegger the gender-neutral term "*das Mensch*," whereas French allows Sartre, as English allows me, only the option between "man" and "woman.") Although Heidegger tends to take a more individualistic perspective in Division Two of *Being and Time*, as he makes clear in the "Letter," ultimately, even our projects are not entirely our own, nor are they simply an artifact of the they-self in which we live, because that they-self has a history and a destiny or fate which is as little under its control as our individual situations are under our control. Harry clearly does not choose for himself the project of destroying Voldemort, neither could he choose it at all if he lived in the muggle world. Similarly, a pre-Hegelian Kierkegaard is hard to imagine. "What throws in projection is not man but Being itself . . ." (BS 241). At the same time, Heidegger validates the method of Division One in the "Letter" by noting that "thinking overcomes metaphysics by climbing back down into the nearness of the nearest" (BW 254), back down into the world of equipment and everydayness.

The latter part of the "Letter" focuses on refuting a series of more general criticisms of Heidegger's work. He argues, among other misunderstandings, that his rejection of humanism is taken as a defense of the inhuman (the original form of this text dates from 1946), his rejection of logic as irrationalism, and his questioning of values in the usual sense as a belief that nothing has value (BW 249). He sees the last point, however, as an assertion of one sort of "value" against another. In fact, his discussion of equipment in *Being and Time* begins with the question of how things can acquire value, with an echo of Hume's implication that this problem is insolvable in ordinary philosophical terms based on perceptual experience (BT 91–92). Instead of reducing values to human emotions, however, as Hume does, in the "Letter," Heidegger moves to the ontological level: "But what a thing is in its Being is not exhausted by its being an object, particularly when objectivity takes the form of value. Every valuing, even where it values positively . . . does not let beings: be" (BW 251). That is, values are human impositions on the reality of what is. One way of formulating Heidegger's ontological humility is precisely "to let beings be."

At the end of the "Letter," Heidegger raises the issues of thinking and of history. In the Prologue, we saw that history (*Geschichte*), as part of our thrownness, is also a destiny (*Geschick*) given or sent to us (to send is *schicken* in German) by Being. In the "Letter," Heidegger rejects his opponents' claim that his work is illogical or irrational by saying that "the destiny of truth, is the first law of thinking—not the rules of logic . . ." He champions thinking against philosophy, because "The thinking that is to come [in the future] . . . thinks more originally than metaphysics—a name identical to philosophy" (BW 264–265). And he traces the source of such thinking in the history of Western thought, and thus in the destiny of the modern world, back to the ancient Greek thinkers who only later came to be known as "philosophers."

The Humility of Ancient Greek Philosophy

> What is amazing about the religiosity of the ancient Greeks is the enormous abundance of gratitude it exudes . . .
>
> —Friedrich Nietzsche, *Beyond Good and Evil*

I

Heidegger taught, and wrote about, ancient Greek philosophy throughout his career, but in this section we will focus on three texts from three different decades of his work. His lectures on Plato's *Sophist* date from 1924 to 1925, when he was writing *Being and Time*; his lectures on Aristotle's *Metaphysics* were given in 1931, soon after it publication; and his lectures on Parmenides in 1942–1943, well into what is called the "later Heidegger." To say that his readings of these texts are nontraditional would be an understatement, but he believes "Ruthlessness toward the tradition is reverence toward the past, and it is genuine only in an appropriation of that latter (the past) out of a destruction of the former (the tradition)" (PS 286). His lectures reflect this and can clearly be seen as an attempt to find in these thinkers the grounds and precursors of his own thought. Yet the lectures are tied, almost word by word at times, to the Greek texts, so they clearly demonstrate the extent to which Heidegger's ontological humility could be said to derive from ancient Greek thought, even if occasionally by devious routes.

Heidegger also traces the denials of our contemporary they-self back to the legacy of ancient Greece. "Precisely in what we no longer see, in what has become an everyday matter, something is at work that was once the object of the greatest spiritual exertions ever undertaken in Western history" (PS 7). This "something" is the understanding of Being. He finds the source of our contemporary equation of both Being and Dasein with beings that are not Dasein in Plato, who achieved "a certain sense of Being . . . [but] it then 'occurred' to him [in the *Sophist*] to express this Being as a being . . ." Heidegger then goes to explain why he sees Aristotle, for whom "a determinate sense of Being guides all his discussions about beings," as closer to the truth than Plato: "Aristotle saw through this peculiar error perfectly, which was quite an accomplishment for a Greek, nearly beyond our power to imagine" (PS 58–59). We can barely imagine this because of the dominance of Plato's "peculiar error" in all subsequent philosophy, until it has become a piece of today's most banal common sense. J. K. Rowling, after all, never reflects on the source of the magic, and its laws, that drive the Harry Potter saga.

In the *Sophist*, possibly the most confounding of Plato's dialogues, the topic of sophistry evolves into the discussion of how one can think about what does not exist. Heidegger says, however, that "The question of [non-being] is ultimately reduced to the question of Being . . ." (PS 299) because Plato casts nonbeing as nothing more than what is different from Being. Moreover, Heidegger argues that, even for the ancient Greeks, "The meaning of Being itself remains unquestioned" and that "The meaning of Being implicitly guiding this ontology is Being = presence" (PS 323). This is the same error *Being and Time* finds in Descartes's work 2,000 years later: "Entities are grasped in their Being as 'presence' . . ." (BT 47). In both texts, Heidegger ties "presence" to the "present-at-hand," the impoverished and derivative way of understanding beings that denies the richness of our experience and cuts objects off from the equipmental totality which gives them meaning. Still, "presence-at-hand" remains the basic understanding of beings in the modern world (PS 119; BT 48)—since time exists, our contemporary understanding of existence in terms of the present-at-hand allows Rowling to represent time as something that could be captured in a bell jar.[10]

Heidegger finds the hidden clue to the true meaning of Plato's *Sophist* near the middle of the dialogue (just as many find the hidden clue to Plato's "Euthyphro" in the reduction of piety to a species of justice near the middle of that dialogue[11]). In the *Sophist* (247e), the Visitor says, "a thing really is if it has any capacity at all, either by nature to do something to something else or to have even the smallest thing done to it by even the most trivial thing, even if it only happens once. I'll take it as a definition that *those which are* amount to nothing other than *capacity* [*dynamis*]."[12] That is, Plato suggests that beings might be defined, not as what is present or present-at-hand to Dasein, as our tradition tells us, but in terms of the ways in which entities affect or are affected by each other. Heidegger notes that "If the traditional interpretation says Plato could not be serious about this definition, that is because [*dynamis*] is translated as 'power,' . . ." whereas Heidegger believes that the correct interpretation is that "Being thus means, put briefly, *possibility* . . ." (PS 328–329).

Heidegger is perhaps his most nontraditional in suggesting that the unaccustomed ontological humility in this passage in Plato shows the influence of his most promising young student, Aristotle. Heidegger bases this on a further claim that Aristotle develops his own concept of *dynamis*, not in isolation as it appears in Plato, but "from the very outset as a category in connection with [*energeia* or actuality[13]]." He finds it "improbable" that Aristotle could have moved from the concept as it appears in Plato to his more robust account, and so concludes that it is his student's early work in this area "which provided Plato the impetus" for his own use of *dynamis* in the *Sophist*. Plato aside, it is clear that this way of understanding Being is one that fascinated Heidegger enough and was closely enough tied to his own developing ontological humility that he devoted a lecture course several years later to the discussion of *dynamis* and *energeia* in Book Theta of Aristotle's *Metaphysics*.[14]

II

Heidegger's work on Aristotle is even more nontraditional than his work on Plato. He begins these lectures by saying, "Aristotle never had in his possession what later came to be understood by the word or the concept 'metaphysics.'"[15] He believes Aristotle came closer to the truth than Plato, because Aristotle does philosophy "not in the sense of a system but in the sense of a task" (AM 10). The contrast with modern philosophy is more emphatic here: "For a long time the erroneous doctrine has existed that being means the same as 'is,' and that the 'is' is said first of all in [logical] judgment. It therefore follows that we first understand being through judgment and assertion. . . . [T]his errant opinion can appeal to the ancients only with partial legitimacy, which means with no legitimacy whatsoever" (AM 21). The ontological humility is also more marked here: "based on Plato's insight [that nonbeing also is], it was once again an equally decisive step for Aristotle to discern that this manifoldness of [B]eing[16] was multistructured, and that this structure had its own necessity" (AM 22). That Being has its own necessity that cannot be reduced to logic or to any other structure of human thought (that is, cannot necessarily be described in language) is the underlying theme of Heidegger's book.

Heidegger considers all the forms the understanding *dynamis* takes in the first section of Book Theta of the *Metaphysics* and concludes that "One might be tempted to say that running through all of these is ability," which for Heidegger means that "philosophy is finished" because the philosophical tradition understands ability by analogy with "Subjective experiences in the internal soul [that] are projected and transferred outward to the objects." That is, philosophy, especially modern philosophy, tends to see things solely in terms of efficient causation, as we have seen, and efficient causation is understood in terms of how humans act on physical objects in the world. Heidegger then shows this is not what Aristotle means by *dynamis* with arguments very similar to those Hume used in his argument about the source of our causal beliefs (AM 61–64).[17] Heidegger concludes that "What is at issue here [with regard to *dynamis*] is not at all a cause-and-effect relationship." Rather, we must understand Aristotle as saying that *dynamis* is "that from out of which change is allowed, or else that from out of which such changes is resisted" (AM 75). As Hagrid repeatedly discovers in the Harry Potter books, not every wild animal can be tamed, and not every seemingly tame animal can be relied on.

What this means is that all beings, not just animals, have their own internal structure which causes, allows, inhibits, or forestalls change. This is their *dynamis*, their "capacity" to change or to remain the same, to be what they are in the way that they are. (Note, again, how this undermines the claim, and the power, of Frye's "arrogant eye" to be able to make of people or things what it chooses.) This is a way of understanding the existence of beings that even sets them outside their roles in the equipmental totalities created by Dasein, much less outside the derivative role of mere presence-at-hand and, as Heidegger says, "lets beings be." He quotes (or interprets) Aristotle as saying that "Having the power for something is properly a force first when it is in the right way," then quickly explains that "right" here "does not mean anything like 'purposeful behavior,' but rather, an inner ordering of something toward an end . . ." (AM 85)—specifically the end or final cause of the being in question. From this he concludes that "Force-being does not consist of two present-at-hand forces," but is the internal relationship between forces for change and what in the object being changed allows or hinders that change (AM 89).

Heidegger next brings Dasein into his account by reinterpreting Aristotle's definition of *anthropos*, usually translated as "rational animal" because of the word *logon*. *Logon* is usually taken to refer to logic or reason, but Heidegger takes it to mean "language," and so reinterprets Aristotle's phrase as "the living being who lives in such a way that his life, as a way to be, is defined in an originary way by the command of language." As already noted, we exist as Dasein only within a social world, which means also a linguistic world. Heidegger's reading of Aristotle not only embodies ontological humility by giving us a way of understanding beings that lets them be, but also by emphasizing the dependence of Dasein on its language and history, on the destiny sent to it by Being. For the ancient Greeks, "Language, therefore, originally and authentically occurs . . . as the proclamation of the world in the invocation of the god" (AM 109).

The last chapter of *Aristotle's Metaphysics* discusses the section of Book Theta on the beliefs of the Megarians, who bear some striking resemblances, in Heidegger's reading, to the modern philosophers discussed in the last chapter. For instance, he contrasts Aristotle's concept of presence with the view of the Megarians, who "comprehend the essence of presence *too narrowly*; they let it be verified and presented only by that which is present in the manner of an [*ergon* or what is actual]" (AM 157–159, his emphasis). He later asks to what extent this definition of presence leads "to the teaching of Protagoras, conceived as the denial of the possible knowledge of beings themselves," because what is perceived is actual "only so long as it is perceived" (AM 171–172). This begins to open the link that we will explore more fully in section three of this chapter between Heidegger's reading of the ancient Greeks and his critique of what he calls "modernity," but it is also important to keep in mind the extent to which he explores the ancients for their own sake. He describes our relationship to them, and to Aristotle in particular, as "an indissolvable bond and an unending obligation" (AM 59).

III

Heidegger begins his lectures on Parmenides, again, by defying tradition, this time the traditional meaning of what it is to know. "What we usually call 'knowing' is being acquainted with something and its qualities . . . Such 'knowledge' seizes the being, 'dominates' it, and thereby goes beyond it and constantly surpasses it." To this he contrasts "essential knowing" which "concerns the being in its ground . . . Essential 'knowing' does not lord it over what it knows but is solicitous toward it." This essential knowing "is a retreat in the face of Being."[18] Based on a much more circumscribed set of available texts than the lectures on Plato and Aristotle, Heidegger nevertheless finds in Parmenides an even deeper understanding of Being, and specifically of the relationship between Being and truth. He then uses these lectures to begin to trace the ways in which the meaning of both Being and truth became hidden and distorted in the history of European thought.

Heidegger does this by "naming" the goddess in verse 22 of the first fragment we have of Parmenides's poem *Alethēia*, the Greek word for truth (P 14). The first thing to be said about this word is that *a* in Greek is a privative prefix, a sign of the absence of what follows, as anonymous means "nameless. The root word is *lethe*, which means forgetting (Lethe is the river of forgetfulness between our world and the underworld in Greek myth). *Alethēia*, or truth, would then literally mean what is not forgotten or unforgotten, but Heidegger defines it as what is "unconcealed." He claims the standard translation makes the Greek concept of truth paradoxical: "If for the Greeks the counter-essence to unconcealedness is falsity and accordingly truth is unfalsity, then concealedness must be determined on the basis of falsity . . . [and] the enigma arises that in the Greek sense the essence of truth receives its character from the essence of falsity" (P 22). His own view is that concealing, not falsity, is primary because we always encounter truth as the unconcealing of what appears in an "open" or a "clearing" against the otherwise hidden background of the everydayness of things.

To take a mundane example, a hammer in use is "concealed," invisible, as we have seen, but becomes visible when it ceases to do its job (because we need to use a screw for the next step in the project instead of a nail, perhaps). Once visible, it opens the question of why it's not doing its job. In this case, the truth that is "unconcealed" is that what looked like a nailing job requires some screws as well. Ron's broken wand in *Harry Potter and the Chamber of Secrets* constantly calls attention to itself in this way, becoming visible against the background of his magical world by not doing what he expects it invisibly to do. On a somewhat higher level, Heidegger tells us in "The Origin of the Work of Art" how Vincent van Gogh's painting of a pair of shoes pulls them out of the concealment of the background and "unconceals" their truth as equipment (BW 158–165).

Heidegger also argues that the "false" is not the opposite of truth in the same way that concealment is. The Greek word is *pseudos*, but Heidegger notes it doesn't mean false in the sense of a false or erroneous proposition, or a false or fake thing. A pseudonym, for instance, both hides the true author and allows him or her to become public (pp. 29–30). Thus, he ultimately concludes that " 'The false,' in the Greek sense, has the basic feature of concealment" (p. 44), as Quirrell conceals Voldemort in his turban in *Harry Potter and the Sorcerer's Stone*, which both hides him and enables his treachery. The Latin root of the word *false*, however, has a different history that, according to Heidegger, relates it to the Romans bringing conquered peoples to a "fall," so that they serve Rome, so that they stand, but not on their own. What is false is not a sham, but what cannot stand, as Peter Pettigrew's masquerade as a pet rat cannot ultimately hide his "true" nature. Heidegger traces the decline he believes follows from this translation of *pseudo* until "the true assumed the character of the not-false" (P 45–46). Truth as the not-false, in turn, becomes the modern concept of truth as correspondence between our beliefs and the way things "really" are. And from that comes the question that plagued Descartes, Hume, Kant, and others: "how is it at all possible for an inner process of the mind or soul to be brought into agreement with things out there?" (P 50–51).

If we have wandered away from Parmenides here, it is because Heidegger does the same, shifting his focus to the ancient Greek concept of truth in general. What he says offers an important insight into his ontological humility, but also requires a fair amount of explanation: "wherever, as well as however, beings let themselves emerge for the Greeks into unconcealedness, there Being is 'put into words.' . . . The proper essence of the word is that it lets beings appear in their Being and preserves what appears, i.e., the unconcealed, as such" (P 76). What he means by this is that language, specifically the naming of things, is what allows us to encounter them as beings of that particular type and to come to know them in relation to other beings and to the human world. Without language, all we find in the world would just be a flux of undifferentiated "stuff." Heidegger believe Parmenides knew this, and we have forgotten it: "The essence of man, as experienced by the Greeks, is determined on the basis of his relation to self-emerging Being, so that man is the one who has the word.[19] And the word is in essence the letting appear of Being by naming" (P 112). Again, the ancient Greeks philosophers still knew how to let beings be.

The Arrogance of Technology

> Only if we become truly humble is the scent awakened for what is great, and only if this occurs do we become capable of wonder. Wonder is, however, the overcoming of the self-evident.
>
> —Martin Heidegger, *Aristotle's Metaphysics* Θ 1–3

I

In *Aristotle's Metaphysics*, Heidegger contrasts Aristotle's views with those of the moderns in several places. He says that Descartes's key question is "How must nature be posited such that it can be recognized scientifically and mathematically" (AM 80). This approach of defining the natural world, not in its own terms, as Aristotle does, or from the perspective of Being, but in terms of human science is, for Heidegger, the founding error of "the technological age." In contrast to the ontological humility he finds in Parmenides and the other great Greek thinkers, Heidegger notes that "Modern man has a 'lived experience' of the world and thinks the world in those terms, i.e., in terms of himself as the being that, as ground, lies at the foundation of all explanation and ordering of beings as a whole" (P 165). In this section we will look at Heidegger's two key texts on "modernity": "The Age of the World Picture" (1938) and "The Question Concerning Technology" (1955). Then we will look at his last works to trace the ontological humility that led him to public silence during the last years of his life.

As noted earlier, large parts of "The Age of the World Picture" were suppressed when it was originally presented during the Third Reich. Here we can see not only the early form of Heidegger's critique of the modern age, but also how far his work already was in 1938 from the kind of thinking that would have been acceptable to the Nazi regime. He begins by listing five characteristics of the modern age: science, technology (which, as we have seen, he considers to be more than merely applied science), art as under "the purview of aesthetics," human activity understood as "culture," and a "loss of the gods" that is compatible with an empty "religiosity" (QT 116–117). All of these point to the fact that we live in the "age of the world picture," by which he means that "What is, in its entirety, is now taken in such a way that it . . . only is in being to the extent that it is set up by man . . ." He sees this way of understanding the world as unique to the modern age, in contrast to the Middle Ages, which understood "that which is" as "that which is created by the personal Creator-God as the highest cause." He also contrasts it with the Greeks, but also says that the Plato's doctrine of forms (*eidos* or Ideas) ". . . is the presupposition, destined far in advance and long ruling indirectly in concealment, for the world's having to become picture" (QT 129–131).

But taking the world as picture changes not only how we see the world, but also how we see ourselves. "There begins that way of being human which [determines] the realm of human capability as a domain given over to measuring and executing, for the purpose of gaining mastery over that which is as a whole." Notice the echoes of Voldemort here, but for Heidegger this describes the humanism he continually rejects as a form of anthropology, which means for him "that philosophical interpretation of man which explains and evaluates whatever is, in its entirety, from the standpoint of man and in relation to man" (QT 132–133). If the world has become a picture, an object that exists only as the object of our perceptions, as he says of the Megarians, then we become correspondingly nothing more than the subject of that perception. That is, we cease to be Dasein engaged in a world that gives our lives life meaning and are reduced to empty perceivers, one kind of being among many, with the sole goal of greater exploitation of the other beings around us.

II

With the image of the world picture as a background, it is easier to understand Heidegger's later account of the decline of the understanding of Being since the time of the ancient Greeks in "The Question Concerning Technology." Here he returns again to Aristotle's understanding of causality, as distinct from the sense of the term we inherit from Descartes. Aristotle identifies four causes necessary to produce something: a formal cause (the form of the thing or the kind of thing it is), a material cause (what it is made out of), a final cause (its purpose or its use, in the case of a human artifact), and an efficient cause (its cause in our sense of the term). We saw in the Prologue how Descartes reduced this four to efficient causality alone, and a narrow focus on efficient causation in Rowling's understanding of magic is one remnant of technological modernity in her books. In his later work Heidegger seeks to revitalize Aristotle's way of understanding how things come to be, labeling them in this text "sky" (formal cause), "earth" (material cause), "gods" (final cause), and "mortals" (efficient causes). Together the four causes are a "bringing forth" of something that he identifies with *poiēsis* (making, but also poetry). This bringing-forth is also a revealing that brings out of concealment (QT 7–11).

The cause(s) of something are what allow it to be revealed out of concealment so that it can be seen as what it truly is. That is, more mundanely, the causes of a living thing such as an oak tree (the acorn, the earth and water that feed it, its evolutionary purpose of producing more acorns, and its own internal mechanisms of growth) allow it to be encountered as an oak tree against the background of the forest and the elements necessary for it to flourish; the causes of an artifact such as a chalice[20] (the silversmith's idea of the chalice, the silver, the Mass where it will be used, and the smith's actions) allow it to be revealed against a background of raw materials, heat, the smith's skill, and the ritual of the Mass. For Heidegger, we know the truth of a object when we understand how it comes to be out of all four causes and what it is in its usefulness to us (the chalice) or its capacity to fulfill its natural purpose (the oak tree). He claims, here and elsewhere, that this way of understanding causality is a way of allowing beings to be.

Technology also reveals, but does so by "challenging" rather than bringing forth. One way to understand "challenging" is in terms of the fact that technology (which Heidegger sees as including all of modern science) can be said to ask questions of the natural (and human) world and demand answers through what we now consider to be scientific method. It searches for the truth of the oak tree by asking how much water and nitrogen it needs to grow, how much carbon dioxide it produces, how many board feet of timber it can be cut into, what its chromosomes look like, and so on. It asks the chalice fewer questions—How pure is its silver? How old is it? Was it made by a famous smith? How much money is it worth?—but only because in the technological age it has no meaning or worth beyond its existence as bare metal or a work of art, both measured in cash value. Science and technology, Heidegger says, reduce everything to "energy that can be extracted and stored as such" (QT 14). His example is the building of a hydroelectric dam that transforms the Rhine River into nothing more than a power source. "Everywhere everything is ordered to stand by, to be immediately at hand, indeed to stand there just so that it may be on call for a further ordering . . . We call it the standing-reserve" (QT 16–17).

Again, however, it is not only the natural world and the world of human artifacts that is challenged in this way. Dasein (which he calls "man" here, since we are firmly in the realm of traditional metaphysics and traditional humanism) also becomes something different, something less in the technological age. "If man is challenged, ordered, to do this, then does not man himself belong, even more originally than nature in the standing-reserve?" Modern philosophy not only fails to distinguish between the being of Dasein and the being of other beings, but provides the philosophical basis for technology, which has the power to make Dasein nothing more than one being among others. This is because Dasein neither controls nor creates any mode of revealing, but only encounters a world that has already been revealed in a determinate way according to how it has been historically and geographically "thrown." The technological age is a natural (but not inevitable) result of how Descartes, and others, reinterpreted the Medieval understanding of Being, just as one could say many of the significant differences between the history of Britain and that of the other nation-states that arose during the same period were the natural (but not inevitable) result of being an island. "Modern technology . . . is, therefore, no merely human doing" (QT 18-19).

Heidegger traces the steps of this transformation in "The Origin of the Work of Art" (1935). There he considers the move from the Greek *hypokeimenon* and *hypostatsis* to the Latin *subiectum* [subject] and *substantia* [substance] and concludes, "*Roman thought takes over the Greek words without a corresponding, equally original experience of what they say, without the Greek word.* The rootlessness of Western thought begins with this translation" (BW 149, his emphasis). He traces this rootlessness in the similar shift from *hyle* and *morphē* to "matter" and "form," and the transition from a Latin to the Christian understanding of the world in which "the totality of all beings is represented in advance as something created, which here means made," or formed, out of some raw material, that is, matter. Moreover, in the Christian view, things are for "man's" use. This understanding of the world carries forward into the modern age, even though it rejects religion because "the theological interpretation of all beings, the view of the world in terms of matter and form . . . having once been instituted, can still remain a force" (BW 155).

All of which leads, without explicit human choice, to the age of technology: "And if form is correlated with the rational and matter with the irrational; . . . if in addition the subject-object relation is coupled with the conceptual pair form-matter; then representation has at its command a conceptual machinery that nothing is capable of withstanding" (BW 153). These Roman-Christian pairings generate a system of hierarchically arranged dualisms that dominate European thought. In Descartes, for instance, it results in the rigid dualism between the rational, knowing subject and the material object of its knowledge discussed in chapter 1. In Hume, we saw the dualism between fact and value, reason and emotion that mirrors Descartes's opposition between mind and body, despite Hume's own skepticism about mental substance.

Form	Matter
Rational	Irrational
Mind	Body
Subject	Object
Humans	Nature

By illuminating the history of these dualisms, Heidegger allows us to see that, while modernity was not inevitable, its path was clearly laid out long ago.

It is here also, however, that we can see another way in which Rowling's story remains itself part of the technological age, the persistence of hierarchical dualisms in her thinking, most obviously the dualism between good and evil and the derivative dualism between arrogance and humility on which this entire project is based. Still, it is notable that many of the dualistic dividing lines increasingly, and intentionally, blur as the Harry Potter saga develops. Sirius tells Harry that "the world isn't split into good people and Death Eaters."[21] The Ministry of Magic, the bastion of anti-Voldemort thinking, facilitates and eventually becomes part of his triumphant return. Conversely, Peter Pettigrew, so much Voldemort's abject slave that he cuts off his own hand to help re-embody the Dark Lord, has toward the end of the saga one kind impulse, which both saves Harry and results in Pettigrew being immediately strangled by the magical prosthetic hand Voldemort created for him.[22] The stories are also heavily marked, as was noted in the Prologue, by what are called luminal or borderline characters, those whose exact place on the line between arrogance and humility (Sirius Black) or good and evil (Snape) can be said to remain ambiguous.

Like Voldemort's arrogance, the end result of the historical process Heidegger describes in "The Question Concerning Technology" is to put humans in mortal danger. He reintroduces the image of the world picture here by naming the challenging of the technological age "Enframing," because it sets everything that is inside a frame to be seen by humans only as standing-reserve. Then, writing in 1949, at the dawn of the Nuclear Age, he says, "The threat to man does not come in the first instance from the potentially lethal machines and apparatus of technology. The actual threat has already affected man in his essence. The rule of Enframing threatens man with the possibility that it could be denied to him to enter into a more original revealing and hence to experience the call of a more primal truth" (QT 28). The gravest danger of technology is not nuclear holocaust or environmental devastation (although these are certainly aspects of it for Heidegger), but the risk that the technological way of revealing, of unconcealing truth, will erase all other ways of understanding the world and cut off our access to any way of letting beings be. At the same time, Heidegger finds in technology, exactly because it is so extreme, what he calls a "saving power" and says, "we are summoned to hope in the growing light of the saving power. How can this happen? Here and now and in little things . . ." (QT 33).

III

By 1964, however, Heidegger's hope seems to have grown dimmer. He says in his last published work, "The End of Philosophy and the Task of Thinking," that philosophy is now at an end because "Philosophy is metaphysics" and "Metaphysics is Platonism." He cautions that this does not mean, as some of analytic philosophers discussed earlier might suggest, that the process by which philosophy since the ancient

Greeks has spun the sciences out of itself has left it with no content of its own.[23] Rather, he suggests that the kind of "thinking" that would replace philosophy would create

> the possibility that the world civilization which is just now beginning may one day overcome the technological-scientific-industrial character as the sole criterion of man's world sojourn. This may happen not of and through itself, but in virtue of the readiness of man for a determination which, whether listened to or not, always speaks in the destiny of man which has not yet been decided. (TB 60)

By contrast to this kind of thinking, "The matter of philosophy as metaphysics is the Being of beings, their presence in the form of substantiality and subjectivity" (TB 62). That is, it understands both Being and Dasein on the model of beings so that they are understood as merely present-at-hand.

Heidegger tells us that the thinking that will replace "philosophy as metaphysics" concerns itself with "what remains unthought in the matter of philosophy . . ." (TB 64). By "unthought" he means the background conditions that make a way of thinking possible without being a directly addressed in it or by it. One could say, for instance, that ontological humility is the unthought in Rowling's saga, or in philosophy itself. What remains unthought in philosophy for Heidegger is first of all Parmenides's goddess, Alethēia, truth as unconcealment. Here, he is more critical of Aristotle's role in the "unthinking" of *alethēia*: "since Aristotle it became the task of philosophy to think beings as such onto-theologically," that is, as we saw above, first as created for "Man" by God and then as objects of perception for technological man, who replaced Him as the center of what is. Heidegger adds, however, that "The reference to what is unthought in philosophy is not a criticism of philosophy."

The question he believes philosophy leaves to thinking is whether, given that "*Alethēia*, unconcealment thought as the opening of presence, is not yet truth," *alethēia* is "then less than truth? Or is it more . . ." (TB 69). In the Prologue we saw that the German for "there is," *es gibt*, translates literally as "it gives." Heidegger concludes this last text by asking, "What speaks in the 'It gives'?" and goes on to end it by saying, "The task of thinking would then be the surrender of previous thinking to the determination of the matter of thinking" (TB 73). What he means by this might be more easily seen in a comment he made a few years earlier about the last line of "The Question Concerning

Technology" that was also quoted in the Prologue, "For questioning is the piety of thought" (QT 25). The translator of that book notes in his Introduction that one of the texts in *On the Way to Language*[24] recalls that line and says, " 'Piety' is meant here in the ancient sense [as] . . . submitting to what thinking has to think about" (QT xxxviii–xxxix). Whatever his failings as a human being, and they were many, in those words Heidegger gives us the definition of ontological humility.

Chapter Three

Existential Humility and Its Other

Sartre

"It is our choices, Harry, that show what we truly are . . ."
—Dumbledore, *Harry Potter and the Chamber of Secrets*

I

We have already seen that one place where Martin Heidegger articulates his ontological humility is in his response to Jean-Paul Sartre's "Existentialism Is a Humanism." In order to see more clearly, therefore, how existentialism can fail to show ontological humility, it seems reasonable to begin with that 1947 article and then work our way backward to Sartre's counterpart to *Being and Time*, namely, *Being and Nothingness* (1943).¹ Unlike Heidegger, Sartre's philosophical position remains fairly consistent across the forty years or so of his philosophical (and literary) career, so there are no complications here of an "earlier" or "later" Sartre. His existentialism developed during the 1930s, was hardened in the fires of the Nazi occupation of France, became one of the shining stars of postwar intellectual life, and remained largely unchanged even in his last works. It is also worth noting that, because of the war, to the extent that his philosophy was influenced by Heidegger, it was by prewar "early" Heidegger, primarily *Being and Time*.

Sartre begins his defense of existentialism with what he calls the "first principle of existentialism": "Man is nothing else but what he makes of himself." Already, we are in some ways much closer here to the work of Descartes than to Heidegger, although Sartre goes on to add, "And when we say that a man is responsible for himself, we do not only mean that he is [in this way] responsible for his own individuality, but that he is responsible for all men"; that is, as he later says, "In choosing myself, I choose man." For Sartre, however, this social aspect of human existence isn't a source of community or even an important aspect of who we are, but rather a primary source of anguish, Angst, because of the burden of being a "lawmaker" for all men.[2] As opposed to the importance of language in Heidegger and the social nature of Dasein, Sartre says that "Subjectivity of the individual is indeed our point of departure, and this for strictly philosophic reasons. . . . There can be no other truth to start from than this: *I think; therefore, I exist.*" He goes on to explain that for him this means "the man who becomes aware of himself through the [Cartesian] *cogito* also perceives all others, and he perceives them as the condition of his own existence. He realizes that he can not be anything . . . unless others recognize it as such" (EE 50–52). We will see later how this yields a social world that is based more on antagonism than on Heideggerian "being with."

Sartre does recognize that we find it necessary "to exist in the world, to be at work there, to be there in the midst of other people," but notes that these limits are both "objective" and "subjective" in the sense that "they are *lived* and are nothing if man does not live them, that is, freely determine his existence with reference to them." This is part of his "humanism"—these "objective" limits have no fixed or intrinsic meaning, are not even limits except insofar as humans freely give them that meaning. One is reminded here of Rowling's Professor Binns, the ghost who was so focused on going to his History of Magic class that he failed to "give meaning" to the fact that his body had died. Freedom to determine the meaning of the "objective" limits, freedom in all its forms is of central importance to Sartre. He says that, "At heart, what existentialism shows is the connection between the absolute character of free involvement . . . and the relativeness of the cultural ensemble which may result from such a choice" (EE 52–53), by which he may not mean that the social world and the "cultural ensemble" it creates is the result of free human choice, but he certainly comes close to saying so.

This should not be entirely surprising, given that he also believes "One may choose anything if it is on the grounds of free involvement," where involvement means, not connection with concrete human others in everyday situation as for Heidegger but the individual's role as lawmaker for all men. For Sartre, humanism can also be understood, not as the "cult" of mankind he attributed to Auguste Comte and to fascism, but as the truth that "there is no lawmaker other than [man], and that in his forlornness he will decide by himself" (EE 60–61). One could easily compare here what Heidegger says in the "Letter," that "in the determination of the humanity of man as [existence] what is essential is not man but Being" (BW 237). Heidegger also says of Sartre's existential humanism in the "Letter" that "if one understands humanism in general as a concern that man become free for his humanity and find his worth in it, then humanism differs according to one's conception of the 'freedom' and 'nature' of man" (BW 225). In the next two sections we will focus specifically on Sartre's conception of those two terms to better understand why he fails to match the ontological humility of Heidegger's work.

II

For Sartre, as for Descartes and Kant, humans exist in the first place as consciousness. His definition in *Being and Nothingness* is that "*consciousness is a being such that in its being, its being is in question in so far as this being implies a being other than itself*" (BN 24). This requires some unpacking because it combines two different views of what consciousness is. The first is Heideggerian: Dasein is unique because "in its Being this being is concerned *about* its very Being" (BW 53, his emphasis). Only an entity that has consciousness can ask questions about its own existence or about Being itself. Sartre's definition of consciousness also includes, however, the definition that is implicit in Descartes and explicit in Hume (although Sartre gets it from Husserl), that consciousness is always consciousness of an object. For Sartre, this is just what consciousness is— "for consciousness there is no being outside of that precise obligation to be a revealing intuition of something" (BN 23). When without any object in any sense, humans are without consciousness, unconscious. On this view, consciousness and its object are given at the same time, but in a "revealing intuition" that seems closer to Descartes seeing the piece of wax as merely "present-at-hand" than to seeing the wax as a piece of ready-at-hand equipment for sealing letters.

Sartre also defines the human by its relationship to Nothingness, although this definition is systematically related to the earlier one (and to his concept of freedom). "Man is the being through whom nothingness comes to the world. But this question immediately provokes another: What must man be in his being in order that through him nothingness may come to being?" The answer to this last question is precisely that humans must be free in order to bring nothingness to the world. Only for a consciousness can something either be or not be. For other beings, what is simply is (BN 59 ff). Sartre says that anguish, Angst, is "the manifestation of freedom in the face of self," not just because of our existence as a lawmaker, but also because "man is always separated by a nothingness from his essence" and so free to re-create himself at any moment (BN 72). Harry Potter constantly returns to the possibility that he might turn out to be like Voldemort, because it is always an open possibility for him. Sartre adds later that we are also separated by a nothingness from what we shall be in the future (BN 75). If, for humans, existence precedes essence, then we never are precisely what we are, but rather are always on the way from what we were, which we are not now, to being what we will become but which we are not yet. For both Sartre and the earlier Heidegger, that is how nothingness enters the otherwise full plenitude of beings that lack this uniquely human trait.

Another way to look at how humans bring nothingness into the world is to note that, while consciousness is always conscious of some object, the object is defined first of all by its not being the consciousness that is conscious of it. Thus, "consciousness is a pure and simple negation of the given." This means that what we are conscious of can never be ourselves as conscious of it. The self we are aware of must always be a past self, a self as Other. This means, as we have seen, that this self is not us and so we are completely free with regard to it, that is, we can at any moment repudiate or negate it. This is the core of Sartre's account of writer Jean Genet—the moment Genet stops stealing and writes *The Thief's Journal*, he ceases to be a thief.[3] "We shall never apprehend ourselves except as a choice in the making. But freedom is simply the fact that this choice is always unconditioned." For Sartre, human freedom is both absolute and central to our existence: "The free project is fundamental, for it is my being." And this free choice is not something that can be done once and for all. Rather, "the project in order to be must be constantly renewed" (BN 615–617). This is another source of existential anguish, Angst, because it underscores that we are not only absolutely free, but also always free to continue on a path or to abandon it.

Of course, Sartre recognizes that "I find myself engaged in an *already meaningful* world which reflects to me meanings which I have not put into it." This social world, however, is not a positive source of meaningful projects, but part of the "coefficient of adversity" created whenever I take on a project, because the world need not promote that project. For Sartre, "my belonging to an inhabited world has the value of a *fact*" (BN 655–656, his emphases) like my past and my (physical) environment. He discusses Heidegger at some length in this context, but concludes that "these external limits of freedom, precisely because they are external . . . will never be either a *real* obstacle for freedom or a limit suffered. Freedom is total and infinite, which does not mean it has no limits but that it *never encounters them*" (BN 680, his emphasis).

Lord Voldemort "dies" with Harry's parents and "dies" again in each of the first two books of the saga (first as Quirrell and then as his own younger self, Tom Riddle), but because he refuses to accept his defeat, he never "encounters" his own death as a limit.

How, one wonders, therefore, can what has no limits, or encounters no limits, maintain its ontological humility? Here, in the relationship between human freedom and the states of affairs in the world in which we live, Sartre's existentialism departs the most from Heidegger and raises important questions about Sartre's work. We will need to look more closely at what Sartre's absolute freedom means with regard to our relationships to the human Other(s) around us and to our own bodies before we turn to how other existentialists deal with the issues of the social world and of our embodiment in ways that come closer to ontological humility.

III

Sartre begins his discussion of the existence of others with an analysis of shame, because "By the mere appearance of the Other, I am put in the position of passing judgment on myself as on an object, for it is as an object that I appear to the Other" (BN 302). From this follows the eeriness of Chapter 21 of *Harry Potter and the Prisoner of Azkaban*, in which Harry and Hermione watch their earlier "Other" selves while waiting for the opportunity to free Sirius from Hogwarts. When the earlier Harry catches a glimpse of his later self, he can only conclude that it is his dead father he has seen, because to other people he looks so much like him. From our perspective, the Other is a being who plays a role in our projects similar (if more unpredictable) to that played by any other object of consciousness. At the same time, we are aware that we have exactly the same status for the Other. For the Other, her projects are paramount, ours relevant only insofar as they impact her. We are each, one might say, only extras in the movie the other one is making about her own life. Shame is our primary reaction because our choices are being seen and judged by standards and needs that are not our own.

Sartre borrows this account, in part, from Hegel, against whose thought Kierkegaard rebelled. Sartre summarized Hegel's "brilliant intuition" as the fact the Hegel realizes, as opposed to Descartes, that I "depend on the Other *in my being* . . . Therefore the Other penetrates me to the heart. I can not doubt him without doubting myself . . ." (BN 321). That is, if there were no Other whom I could know to be not myself, I could not know myself as consciousness either—there would just be a single, unbroken consciousness, only one way of seeing the world, and hence no "way" of seeing the world, just the world as it is for me (which returns us to Descartes's occasional flirtation with equating himself with God).

Another way of understanding this is in terms of the "for-itself," a way of referring to human consciousness that the early Heidegger, Sartre, and Hegel share. Human existence is "for-itself" because it is conscious of its own existence as such, as opposed to the "in-itself," which has a fixed essence and so just is what it is. But I can exist "for myself" only if I have some concept of what it would be to exist for another, if I am aware of my existence as opposed to another's: "I am unable to bring about any relation between what I am in the intimacy of the For-Itself, without distance, without recoil, without perspective, and this unjustifiable being-in-itself which I am for the Other" (BN 362). The Other, by seeing me as an object in her world, gives me an essence which I am not for myself, but which I am for her, thereby alienating me from myself as I know myself to be (that is, free). To take the example of Genet again, he is seen by the Other as a thief first, and only chooses to become a thief later in an act of free defiance. Sartre insists that this dialectic of self and Other must always be seen from the perspective of the self, so that "I must establish myself *in my being* and posit the Other in terms of my being. In a word, the sole point of departure is the interiority of the [Cartesian] *cogito*" (BN 329, his emphasis).

For Sartre, therefore, my primary relationship to the Other is adversarial, because we both want the world to be organized solely from our own points of view. "The appearance of the Other . . . causes the appearance in the situation of an aspect which I did not wish, of which I am not master, and which on principle escapes me because it is *for the Other*" (BN 355, his emphasis). At the same time, the Other is encountered only as another consciousness because "The Other is in no way given to us as an object" (BN 359), since an object could not redefine the world in this way. Rather than living first in a social world and then, in a moment of Angst and authenticity, choosing one's existence, as in Heidegger, for Sartre, the relation to the Other is first of all abstract and theoretical, and only later empirical and concrete. He says that "the appearance of a man as an object in my field of experience is not what informs me that *there are* [here] men. My certainty of the Other's existence is independent of these experiences and is, on the contrary, that which makes them possible" (BN 373). For him, "The being-for-others precedes and founds the *being-with-others*" (BN 537). Sartre affirms freedom by ridding us of the concrete human bonds, and human meanings, that might interfere with it, but then leaves us in anguish at the meaninglessness of the freedom this move generates.

Sartre's emphasis on consciousness as the "'nature' of man" creates a problem not only for how we relate to other people, but also for how we can understand the relationship between our existence as free for-itself and the in-itself object that is our physical body. He discusses three "ontological" dimensions of the body: that "I exist as my body," that "My body is known and utilized by the Other," and that "I exist for myself as a body known by the Other" (BN 460). To unpack these in order, I exist as my body because my body is the means through which I carry out projects in the world. It is, one might say, consciousness operationalized. "The body is the instrument which I am" (BN 470), he says, although he leaves open whether it is the sort of instrument used in an operating room or the kind a musician might use, that is, whether it is a purely external means to achieve our goals or an intrinsic part of our projects. We have already seen how my body exists as the medium of my relationship with others, and vice versa. And finally, note that he ties our existence as body in the third ontological dimension to the knowledge, not the lived experience, of others. To regain a living social world, a lived body, and a corresponding sense of ontological humility, it seems existentialism must go beyond Sartre's formulations.

Beauvoir

> The method defined here acknowledges the feeling that all true knowledge is impossible. Solely appearances can be enumerated and the climate make itself felt.
>
> —Albert Camus, "The Myth of Sisyphus"

I

Simone de Beauvoir is perhaps most famous as the author of *The Second Sex* (1949),[4] the groundbreaking text that founded what is now known as second-wave feminism, but here we will focus on her other major philosophical work, *The Ethics of Ambiguity* (1947). In order to do that, however, it will first be necessary to offer a brief account of those portions of Albert Camus's existentialist classic "The Myth of Sisyphus" (1942) to which Beauvoir's text is, in part, a response. Camus's text will also provide concrete examples of the often abstract concepts at play here, and a bridge between Sartre's individualism and Beauvoir's more socially embedded version of existentialism.

The question asked, and answered in the negative, in "The Myth of Sisyphus" is whether, given the absurdity of human existence, suicide is justified. By the absurd, Camus means those aspects of human life that generate Angst—the fact that time, rather than being the physical dimension we usually think of it as, depends on human consciousness; the extent to which the in-itself is alien to human projects and aspirations; the human Other; our own embodiment; and our own inevitable death.[5] These facts are not themselves absurd, however. Rather they reflect the failure of the world to meet our expectation that it should make sense. The absurd "is the confrontation of this irrational [world] and the wild longing for clarity whose call echoes in the human heart. The absurd depends as much on man as on the world" (MS 21). In this lies the answer to the question about suicide. Just because the absurd requires both an irrational world and the human demand for reason, suicide is "acceptance at its extreme," it is a surrender to irrationality that obliterates the absurd situation at the same time it destroys a human life. Instead, we must defy our fate and refuse suicide (MS 54–55). From this refusal, Camus draws three "consequences": revolt, freedom, and passion (MS 64). He then gives us three ways of living that embody each of these as models of his vision of the existential life.

He matches these lives, however, with revolt, freedom, and passion in unexpected ways. He first links the Don Juan to revolt rather than passion. The source of Don Juan's revolt is his awareness that "There is no noble love but that which recognizes itself to be both short-lived and exceptional" (MS 74) and that, therefore, all the myriad rules meant to keep him from acting on that awareness, all of society's efforts to hide that Angst-inducing truth from us, must be disregarded, overturned, and destroyed. (But note that Camus ignores the consequences of Don Juan's rule-breaking for his female partners, which in Don Juan's time could have been catastrophic.) The life of freedom is that of the actor, who freely becomes now one person, now another as his profession requires. "He abundantly illustrates every month or every day that so suggestive truth that there is no frontier between what a man wants to be and what he is. Always concerned with better representing [the lives of others], he demonstrates to what degree appearing creates being" (MS 79). Finally, passion is captured in the life of the conqueror, who acts in history knowing that history and death will eventually crush him. Unlike Voldemort, the conqueror knows his victories are ultimately pointless because "there is but one victory, and it is eternal [life]. That is the one I shall never have" (MS 87). The conqueror's passion is to devote his life to building an empire that, like Ozymandias's, can only fade into the sands of time.

There is also a fourth life in "The Myth of Sisyphus," that of the writer (or other creative artist). For Camus, "the absurd joy par excellence is creation" (MS 93), because, like the conqueror the artist constantly battles to create what can only be destroyed, like the actor he knows "there is no frontier between being and appearing" (MS 117), and like Don Juan, he must begin over and over again to achieve his unachievable goal of pure love, pure living, pure action. Despite its lyrical beauty and poignant images of the limits of human existence, however, what separates Camus's thought from Beauvoir, and from ontological humility, is the emphasis on revolt and defiance as a response to the absurd. Camus's defiance seems almost to suggest that humans are entitled to better than we receive from the world or from fate. But on what basis? If we are, as Heidegger says, thrown projection, how can we argue that the absurdity of the world is a lack, either in it or in ourselves, without assuming, in a move that Sartre and Camus both imply but would both strongly reject, that we should be masters of a world created to suit our needs so that it makes sense to us? Camus has the nostalgic air, not of someone who is "logical to the bitter end" (MS 9), but of a spurned lover when he says that "There is no fate that cannot be surmounted by scorn" (MS 121).

II

Beauvoir's begins *The Ethics of Ambiguity* by echoing the Sartrean themes of death and nothingness. She quotes Michel de Montaigne's saying that we are born to die, then adds that "Man knows and *thinks* this tragic ambivalence which the animal and the plant merely undergo," and "escapes from his natural condition without, however, freeing himself from it." Not only is death inevitable, but as in Camus, time itself reveals the emptiness of what we are: "between the past which no longer is and the future which is not yet, this moment when he exists is nothing." She argues that ethics has traditionally suppressed this truth and based itself on an assumed human essence, either a pure consciousness beyond the empirical world (as in Kant) or a rational animal guided by pleasure and pain (as in Hume's Utilitarianism). "It has been a matter of eliminating the ambiguity by making oneself pure inwardness or pure externality, by escaping from the sensible world or being engulfed in it." Since we exist as both consciousness and (animal) embodiment, her project is "to assume our fundamental ambiguity. It is in the knowledge of the genuine conditions of our life that we must draw our strength to live and our reason for acting." After all, "One does not offer an ethics to a God."[6]

She draws several conclusions from adopting an existentialist attitude. The first is that "man will not agree to recognize any foreign absolute" imposed from without, but will choose and thereby make his own values. "But," she asks, "if man is free to define for himself the conditions of a life which is valid in his own eyes, can he not choose whatever he likes and act however he likes? Dostoievsky [*sic*] asserted, 'If God does not exist, everything is permitted'" (EA 15), a sentiment Voldemort sometimes seems to echo. Heidegger, Sartre, and Camus all ask the same question, but Beauvoir's answer is somewhat different: "for existentialism, it is not impersonal universal man who is the source of values, but the plurality of concrete, particular men projecting themselves toward their ends." For her, "An ethics of ambiguity will be one which will refuse to deny *a priori* that separate existents can, at the same time, be bound to each other, that their individual freedoms can forge laws valid for all" (EA 17–18). However, she interprets this Kantian dictate in an unusual way. Taking human freedom as a starting point, she proclaims that our freedom "is the source from which all significations and all values spring. It is the original condition of the justification of existence." Only because we are free can we have values or any morality. This becomes the basis for her ethics.

She does this, however, on the background of lives not freely lived. These include what she terms the "infantile" life in which people "can exercise their freedom, but only within this universe which has been set up before them, without them." She puts in this category not only children, but also slaves and, in an echo of *The Second Sex*, "women in many civilizations" who "can only submit to the laws, the gods, the customs, and the truths created by the males" (EA 37), a Don Juan's lovers submitted to his truth. When, in the ideal course of things, adolescents of whatever gender realize their freedom relative to the values and projects of their parents, generally in a moment of Angst, they must choose whether to exercise that freedom or, as in Heidegger, deny it and adopt the values of what Beauvoir calls "the serious" (EA 44). "The serious" is the realm of Kierkegaard's Ethical and, on a less elevated plane, of Harry Potter's muggle family, the Dursleys, and of Ron Weasley's self-important older brother Percy. In another echo of *The Second Sex*, Beauvoir says this choice for or against "the serious" is not determined by biological sex or bodily characteristics, because the body "is not a brute fact. It expresses our relationship to the world. . . . And on the other hand, it *determines* no behavior" (EA 41, her emphasis). As in Sartre, the body has and can act on only the meanings we give to it.

For Beauvoir, those who remain infantile when they actually are free and choose to live in "the serious world" are dangerous because they actively deny their freedom by a total commitment to the values they see themselves as forced to adopt. Moreover, the serious man "ignores the value of the subjectivity and the freedom of others" (EA 49). The "demoniacal man" is the inverse of the serious man, someone who affirms the values of the serious world by a revolt that simply negates them in an illusory imitation of true freedom (EA 53). There are aspects of the demoniacal in Sirius Black (who while at Hogwarts played a potentially fatal prank on Snape, his classmate) and in Peeves, the poltergeist at Hogwarts who disrupts things just for the sake of disruption, as well as, of course, in Voldemort and his followers, who call themselves "Death Eaters" because they live from the death of those they deem unworthy of life.

Beauvoir follows these three negative "types" (infantile, serious, and demoniacal) with three more positive lives, very similar to those found in Camus, who also have not yet achieved ontological humility. The conqueror has become the adventurer who refuses to "attach himself to the end at which he aims; only to his conquest. He likes action for its own sake. He finds joy in spreading through the world a freedom which remains indifferent to its content" (EA 58). The problem with the adventurer is that "he thinks he can assert his own existence without taking into account that of others," and she refers here to both the conquistador Pizarro's attitude toward the Incas and Don Juan's toward Elvira (EA 61). The "passionate man," by contrast, "sets up the object as an absolute not, like the serious man, as a thing detached from himself, but as a thing disclosed by his subjectivity." While many artists would fall into this category, ultimately the passionate man is less an artist than a lover who falls in love with and wants to control his own creation, failing to see that love is "the renunciation of all possession . . ." (EA 67). True artists show more ontological humility and do not "propose to attain being . . . It is existence which they are trying to pin down and make eternal" (EA 69). Their passion is not for the work as a finished object, but for the creative process itself insofar as it mirrors the ambiguity of the human situation.

The ethical conclusion Beauvoir draw from all this is that "Freedom must project itself toward its own reality through a content whose value it establishes. . . . But this implies that freedom is not to be engulfed in any goal; neither is it to dissipate itself vainly without aiming at a goal." The adventurer's goal is freedom for himself; the passionate man's goal is an object that consumes him. Both are flawed because "freedom cannot will itself without aiming at an open future." And because human freedom is always freedom in a social context, this means further that "every man needs the freedom of other men," because "Man can find a justification of his own existence only in the existence of other men." For Beauvoir, this is simply a more concrete form of the Kantian dictate that "To will oneself free is also to will others free," albeit embedded in a very different metaphysical, and ontological, world (EA 71–73).

III

Beauvoir's philosophy clearly demonstrates ontological humility in at least two ways. The first is reflected in the quotation in the Prologue where she says politicians must always ask, "Am I really working for the liberation of men? Isn't this end contested by the sacrifices through which I aim at it?" (EA 133–134). This humility arises out of the resistance to the Nazi occupation of France and the loss of friends and former students in a cause she encouraged them to serve. It arises as well out of the postwar struggles against colonial oppression, which also taught that resisting oppression can be dangerous. If that resistance becomes violent, the danger is multiplied, even more so if it is armed resistance. For philosophers who promote resistance, and those who instigate or lead it, there is a price: "one finds himself forced to treat certain men as things in order to win the freedom of all."

The battle for freedom requires sacrifices, not all of them voluntary. "We are obliged to destroy not only the oppressor but also those who serve him, whether they do so out of ignorance or out of constraint." Worse, we must also sacrifice "those who are fighting on our side, and even ourselves" (EA 97–99). Worse yet is the inevitability of what is now called "collateral damage"—"every struggle obliges us to sacrifice people whom our victory does not concern, people who, in all honesty, reject it as a cataclysm: these people will die in astonishment, anger or despair" (EA 108). From the death of Cedric Diggory in the fourth Harry Potter book to the death of Dobby and many, many others in the last one, the collateral damage in Rowling's saga is high, but always marked and grieved. The result of this complexity in moral choices even for an obvious good, Beauvoir underscores, is to undermine utterly any easy self-satisfaction one might feel in acting to achieve one's own freedom or to bring freedom to others.

This is one of several places where Beauvoir argues against any Utilitarian justification based on a claim that the costs of resistance are outweighed by the good it achieves. She continually reminds us that "Such a position would be solid and satisfactory if the word *useful* had an absolute meaning in itself." She agrees with Kant that transcendent values exist, but underscores that they exist as willed by human beings in the course of the ethical decisions that they make. Against Mill she argues that what is useful is dependent on the human projects it serves. She rejects the idea that there can be something that is useful in general because it is useful to humankind as a whole, since "the terms 'useful to Man,' 'useful to this man,' do not overlap." She concludes that "in order to serve some men we must do disservice to others. By what principle do we choose between them?" (EA 111–113).

Her answer to this last question is not in terms of the numbers on each side of the equation, as it would be for Mill's Utilitarianism. Rather, she finds a guide in the potential for freedom that is created by the sacrifice being made: "the complement of the word *useful* is the word *man*, but it is also the word *future*" (EA 115). This is where the two sides of the ontological humility referred to above articulate with each other. She notes that "whatever may be the philosophy we adhere to . . . the practical attitude remains the same; we must decide upon the opportuneness of an act and attempt to measure its effectiveness without knowing all the factors that are present" (EA 122–123). We always act out of necessary ignorance, and so our acts can never be fully justified, yet they are necessary and necessarily directed at freedom.

Beauvoir goes on to develop an elaborate and illuminating set of analogies between such choices and, on the one hand, scientific experiments and, on the other hand, artistic creation. She continues the above discussion with the comment that "A choice of this kind is no more arbitrary than a hypothesis; it excludes neither reflection nor even method; but it is also free, and it implies risks that must be assumed as such" (EA 123). She later brings art into the discussion by saying, "failure and success are two aspects of reality which at the start are not perceptible. That is what makes criticism so easy and art so difficult. . . ." One similarity between art and science is that they "do not establish themselves despite failure but through it." The battle for freedom, she argues, achieves freedom in the very act, just as art exists only "because at every moment art has willed itself absolutely," that is, as we saw, the object of true artistic creation is not the work, but the creation of it (EA 129–131). She concludes that "Ethics does not furnish recipes any more than do science and art. One can merely propose methods" (EA 134).

The method Beauvoir proposes owes much to Kant: "the individual as such is one of the ends at which our action must aim" (EA 135). Still, she adds new dimensions to this line of moral reasoning. One is joy: "in order for the idea of liberation to have a concrete meaning, the joy of existence must be asserted in each one, at every instant; the movement toward freedom assumes its real, flesh and blood figure in the world by thickening into pleasure, into happiness" (EA 135). A more important added dimension is the recognition that "The Other is multiple, and on the basis of this new questions arise." This raises the moral and political stakes because "each finite undertaking must also be open on [the freedom of] the totality of men" (EA 144). Beauvoir adds to Sartre's absolute freedom the corollary that we find the law of our freedom in that freedom itself. Man, first, "must assume his freedom and not flee it; he assumes it by a constructive movement; one does not exist without doing something; and also by a negative movement which rejects oppression for oneself and for others" (EA 156). She reminds us that "one never realizes anything but a limited work" (EA 158). The ambiguity of the human situation means that all action is necessarily incomplete and leaves it with no final justification. Earlier she quoted the French revolutionary Saint-Just: "No one governs innocently" (EA 108). Perhaps that is one reason Dumbledore refused to ever become the Minister of Magic.

Merleau-Ponty

> The real is a closely woven fabric. It does not await our judgement before incorporating the most surprising phenomena, or before rejecting the most plausible figments of our imagination.
> —Maurice Merleau-Ponty, *Phenomenology of Perception*

I

Merleau-Ponty is less well-known than his colleagues at the influential postwar periodical *Les Temps Modernes*, but his philosophy both adds new dimensions of ontological humility to their thought and can serve as a useful transition between existentialism and the thinkers discussed in the next chapter. Where Beauvoir can be seen to add an essential element of social embeddedness to the existentialism of Sartre and Camus, Merleau-Ponty focuses primarily on the relationship between free consciousness[7] and the limits of the concrete human body that opens other doors for feminist thought.[8] His work, like Heidegger's, can be divided into an earlier period with *Phenomenology of Perception* (1947) at its core, and a later one that reflects a shift in perspective found primarily in his unfinished work, *The Visible and the Invisible* (1959–1961). We will look at these two works in turn as we move toward what is called postmodern thought, but both begin from the idea that our body is how we carry out projects in the world and the basic existentialist insight that

> I am the absolute source, my existence does not stem from my antecedents, from my physical and social environment;

instead it moves out towards them and sustains them, for I alone bring into being for myself . . . the tradition which I elect to carry on, or the horizon whose distance from me would be abolished—since that distance is not one of its properties—if I were not there to scan it with my gaze. (PP ix)

On this basis, Merleau-Ponty reaches a new understanding of what consciousness is.

He starts by rejecting both the Empiricist account of perception and the Cartesian/Kantian "intellectualism" that reduces experience to the raw material of rational processes. In discussing attention, he notes that "Empiricism cannot see that we need to know what we are looking for, otherwise we would not be looking for it, and intellectualism fails to see that we need to be ignorant of what we are looking for, or equally again we should not be searching" (PP 28). Rowling's descriptions of how Harry searches for the snitch when paying seeker in a Quidditch match are excellent examples of this. He scans his visual field while in constant motion to locate something that, because it is in constant rapid motion as well, will always have moved somewhere else relative to him as soon as he sees it, yet he has the visual and bodily skill to find and usually catch it. Merleau-Ponty's much more abstract account is that we search for an object that is in our perceptual field, but not yet explicit there, so it is both known as latently present and unknown as "fully determinate object" (PP 49), that is, in Harry Potter's case, as a snitch in a specific location.

The underlying paradox is that "Our perception ends in objects, and the object once constituted appears as the reason for all the experiences of it which we have had or could have" (PP 67). That is, when we see an object it seems to be what it is independently of our perceptions of it. Merleau-Ponty unpacks the perceptual process to reveal the active role that consciousness plays in it, while at the same time revealing the dependence of consciousness on the body. Based on the research of the early Gestalt psychologists, he replaces the image of an inert body moved through some causal chain by consciousness to that of the "phenomenal body" which is the action of our consciousness in the world (PP 106). He also describes the "intentional arc," a structure that supports this consciousness and "projects around about us our past, our future, our human setting, our physical, ideological and moral situation, or rather which results in our being situated in all these respects," that is, situated in an already meaningful world (PP 136). This is so to such an extent that "movement and background are, in fact, only artificially separated stages of a unique totality" (PP 138). When I walk across a room or reach for a pen, I don't experience empty space, but move toward my goal along the lines of access (distance, obstacles) that the intentional arc reveals in that space, just as Harry Potter organizes the visual field of a Quidditch match as the space for the appearance of the snitch he is looking for.

For Merleau-Ponty this means that "Bodily experience forces us to acknowledge an imposition of meaning . . . which clings to certain contents" (PP 147). Some of these imposed meanings arise from the body itself. One example of this is our sexuality (in itself, arguably, a proto-feminist choice of topics[9]), which "without being the object of any intended act of consciousness, can underlie and guide specific forms of my experience" (PP 169) as a gendered being in a social world. We encounter the body the same way we encounter the social world, as always already there and as a source of meanings we did not create. At the same time, "The subject of sensation is neither a thinker who takes note of a quality, nor an inert setting which is affected or changed by it, it is a power which is born into, and simultaneously with, a certain existential environment . . ." (PP 211). I am my body, but my body is not a machine—it is the presence of my consciousness in the world. As such it both allows me to act in the world, and limits the mode and scope of my actions by the interaction between its material existence and the material things around me. To walk across a room, I "use" my body, but can only do so in ways unique to my body and the specific "intentional arc" I am suspended in as a being in the world.

Merleau-Ponty's reliance on psychological studies sometimes leads him to conclusions that may appear to be strange, but reveal deep truths about our experience of the world. He says, for instance, "What protects the sane man against delirium or hallucination is not his critical powers, but the structure of his space . . ." (PP 291). In part, this refers to the fact that normal perception occurs in an anonymous perceptual space that is available to others, while a hallucination does not. It also means, however, that "Perceiving is putting one's faith, at a stroke, in a whole future of experiences, and doing so in a present which never strictly guarantees the future; it is placing one's belief in a world," which is something the delirious or hallucinating perceiver cannot do. This is not to say that perception is never wrong—"There is the absolute certainty of the world in general, but not of any one thing in particular" (PP 297). As Merleau-Ponty explains, "I perceive a thing because I have a field of existence and because each phenomenon, on its appearance, attracts toward that field the whole of my body as a system of perceptual powers" (PP 318). Even perceptual errors are judged against the whole perceptual field, and only in this way can they be seen to be errors. Hallucinations, by contrast, deprive the perceiver of an anchoring world by which they can be known to be illusions. First I have a world, and only then do I have the perceptions that make up that world. "I know myself only in so far as I am inherent . . . in the world, that is, I know myself only in my ambiguity" (PP 345).

II

This bodily existence is what situates us in a social world in which we live among others: "We must therefore rediscover, after the natural world, the social world, not as an object or sum of objects, but as a permanent field or dimension of existence. . . . Our relationship to the social is, like our relationship to the world, deeper than an express perception or any judgement."

Merleau-Ponty also notes that "the social does not exist as a third person object" (PP 362). The body opens us to a world that is not only inherently "anonymous" and available to others, but also rich with the meanings that others, individually and collectively, have given to it. (Harry and Hermione, raised by muggles, must explicitly learn the social meanings of the "wizarding world.") Others exist as a necessary background or horizon against which my own life, my own projects can have meaning. "In short, just as the instant of my death is a future to which I have not access, so I am necessarily destined never to experience the presence of another person to himself. And yet each other person does exist for me as an unchallengeable style or setting of co-existence, and my life has a social atmosphere just as it has a flavour of mortality" (PP 364). Both thrownness and projection are necessarily linked to our existence among others.

This necessity of a social world, however, serves to re-embed us in our bodies because "unless I have an exterior others have no interior." My body is not only what gives me access to the world, but also what allows me to know that other bodies also bring other consciousnesses into that world. If I controlled my world and my meanings (an illusion which, as Beauvoir, Frye, and many others have noted, is far easier for men to maintain in our society than women), I would have no reason to believe that my body or any other consciousnesses exist. In fact, as we saw with regard to Descartes: "It is ultimately with God that the *cogito* brings me into coincidence" (PP 373). Merleau-Ponty argues that "it is not *because* I think that I am certain of my existence; on the contrary the certainty I enjoy concerning my thoughts stems from their genuine existence" (PP 382). If we start with the thoughts, as Hume does, however, we never arrive back at a substantial self because "the presence of oneself to oneself, being no less than existence, is anterior to any philosophy, and knows itself only in those extreme situations in which it is under threat: for example in the dread of death or of another's gaze upon me" (PP 404). To avoid Hume's problem, we must move not back but outward, toward the social and perceptual world that grounds our existence.

Merleau-Ponty keeps existential freedom, but situates it in the world. In an oblique reference to Camus, he says, "It is not within my power to be a warrior or seducer with ease and in a way that 'comes naturally'; really to *be* one" because we cannot really *be* anything. We can act the part and in so doing create ourselves, but only partially and provisionally. Even that, however, proves our freedom because "what are called obstacles to freedom are really deployed by it." My freedom to be a warrior is only denied if I make it my project to be a warrior; otherwise those aspects of my existence that make it impossible mean nothing. And the choice to be or not be a warrior is always reversible, as Neville Longbottom learns in *Harry Potter and the Deathly Hallows*. For Merleau-Ponty, "the real choice is that of whole character and our manner of being in the world" (PP 436–437). He seeks to balance freedom and necessity: "here once more we must recognize a sort of sedimentation in our life. . . . Yet since freedom does not tolerate any motive in its path, my habitual being in the world is at each moment equally precarious" (PP 441). Following the well-worn path of my life is as much an exercise of freedom as deciding to remake myself as a warrior.

Freedom, he tells us, exists in the fact that "The world is already constituted, but also never completely constituted; in the first case we are acted upon, in the second we are open to an infinite number of possibilities." The important thing is that "we exist in both ways *at once*" (PP 453, his emphasis). That phrase is the hallmark of both Merleau-Ponty's method and his conclusions in his early work, and of his ontological humility. We exist as body and consciousness, alone *and* with others, as free *and* as limited. This follows from the very fact of our embodiment: "Nothing determines me from outside, not because nothing acts on me, but, on the contrary, because I am from the start outside myself and open to the world," that is, as consciousness the world is given with my perception of it. In his one clear reference to ethics in this book, he says there is no theoretical answer to the moral questions he poses, but "there is before you this person whom you love, there are these men whose existence around you is that of slaves, and *your* freedom cannot be willed without leaving behind its singular relevance, and without willing freedom *for all*." He ends with a quotation from Antoine de Saint-Exupéry: "Man is but a network of relationships, and these alone matter to him" (PP 456).

III

At the time of his death, Merleau-Ponty was engaged in a project that, while not discontinuous with his earlier work, was clearly leading his thought in a new direction. In *The Visible and the Invisible* he begins with perception, but with a section titled "The Perceptual Faith and Its Obscurity."[10] The obscurity of perception comes in part from the fact that we are already, as body, present in a perceptual field and a social world we cannot control or completely know. "I am in every operation of knowledge delivered over to an organization of my thoughts whose premises are masked from me" (VI 43). These premises come in part from my existence among things where "there is a profusion of perspectives which are not as nothing and which oblige me to say that the thing itself is always further on" (VI 77), because I never have a total and complete perception of it. They also come from my existence among others. Harry Potter's tie to Voldemort is as much a brute fact for him as the scar on his forehead. "It is necessary and it suffices that the other's body which I see and his word which I hear, which are given to me as immediately present in my [perceptual] field, *do present to me in their own fashion what I will never be present to*, what will always be invisible to me" (VI 82, his emphasis). Theses premises come, in short, from the body, from time, from history, which he characterizes here not as backgrounds or horizons, as in his earlier work, but as "mists" that "enshroud" our life (VI 84).

As opposed to Sartre's insistence that human existence opens a nothingness in the plenitude of the world, Merleau-Ponty gives an affirmation of ontological humility:

> The effective, present, ultimate and primary being, the thing itself, are in principle apprehended in transparency through their perspectives, offer themselves therefore only to someone who . . . limits himself to giving them the hollow, the free space they ask for in return, the resonance they require, who follows their own movement, who is therefore not a nothingness the full being would come to stop up but a question consonant with the porous being which it questions and from which it obtains not an *answer*, but a confirmation of its astonishment. (VI 101–102)

Astonishment and questioning are key here, as is the need to respond to "the things themselves" in the terms that they provide without expecting full or final answers. In real life, Dumbledore doesn't show up to explain everything in the final chapter. This view is based on Merleau-Ponty's understanding of perception and the body because "The visible can thus fill me and occupy me only because I who see it do not see it from the depths of nothingness, but from the midst of itself; I the seer am also visible" (VI 113). A disembodied consciousness might be God, but a blind God who could know its Creation but would have no viewpoint from which to see it.

Although Merleau-Ponty discusses language in *Phenomenology of Perception*, it takes on a new prominence here as a kind of second body. He says this relationship between language and the body is "much more than a parallel or an analogy . . . there is solidarity and intertwining" based on how both are ways in which consciousness acts in and is acted on by the world. "Like the flesh of the visible, speech is a total part of the significations, like it, speech is a relation to Being through a being, and, like it, it is narcissistic, eroticized, endowed with a natural magic that attracts the other significations into its web, as the body feels the world in feeling itself" (VI 118). My pen exists in an "equipmental totality," as Heidegger says, of paper, desk, books, editors, readers, and, so the word "pen" draws all of those other words in its wake, as well as its own image in the mind and, more vaguely, the other significations that form the shadows of its sound and shape, the pencil, the plume, but also the animal enclosure, the prison cell. Words have their own materiality that links us up with our environment in ways much like, but quite different than. the ways our body situates us in it. In neither case, however, is there any mastery by a pure (and stereotypically masculine) consciousness.

In fact, each of these penumbras that shadow our existence has its own uniqueness: "the past and the present, the essence and the fact, space and time, are not *given* in the same sense, and none of them is given in the sense of coincidence" (VI 124). This last point is important because part of his argument is that "metaphysics is coincidence," that is, relies on the real and full presence of beings to our knowing minds. "That there is this thickness of flesh between us and the 'hard core' of Being, this does not figure in the definition . . ." (VI 127). For Merleau-Ponty, there is no such coincidence—there is intertwining, of consciousness and body, of seer and seen, of self and Other, of word and thing, of present, past, and future. Toward the end of this unfinished work, he asks a question prompted by the importance he now gives to language. He asks "[B]y what miracle a created generality, a culture, a knowledge [might] come to add to and recapture and rectify the natural generality of my body and of the world" (VI 152), but offers no answer to the question in this unfinished final work.

The last part of *The Visible and the Invisible* consists of "Working Notes." Here we can see the extent to which ontological humility became central to Merleau-Ponty's thinking, and the extent to which he was influenced by the innovations in linguistics that led to the reconfiguration of philosophy discussed in the next chapter. He notes, for instance, the claim of structural linguistics discussed below that "There are only *differences* between significations" (VI 171); he also uses much more of Heidegger's terminology than in his published work. He insists that "I do not perceive any more than I speak—Perception has me as has language" (VI 190). Some comments are critical of *Phenomenology of Perception* (VI 200), some of *The Visible and the Invisible* itself: "there is all the same this difference between perception and language, that I *see* the perceived things and that the significations on the contrary are invisible . . . The Being whose home is language cannot be fixed, looked at, it is only from afar . . ." (VI 214). Most important, however, is his growing awareness that "consciousness," which was central to existentialism, must be replaced by "fields in intersection" (VI 227), as it will be in postmodern thought.

Chapter Four

Postmodern Humility and Its Other

Foucault

Maybe the target nowadays is not to discover what we are, but to refuse what we are.

—Michel Foucault, "The Subject and Power"

I

Several ways could be found to describe the intellectual commonalities between the work of Michel Foucault and that of Jacques Derrida. Despite the limitations of the term, I have chosen the word "postmodern" because these two thinkers clearly operate in an intellectual space beyond and based on Heidegger's critique of modernity as laid out in "The Question Concerning Technology" and "The Age of the World Picture." Moreover, Foucault himself uses the image of the picture, specifically Diego Velázquez's *Las Meniñas* (1656), as an entrée into his account of the beginnings of modernity in his book *The Order of Things*. There he notes, among several other unusual features of the painting, that the focal point of the canvas is not one of the paintings on the background wall, but rather a mirror. Reflected in the mirror are the images of King Philip IV of Spain and his queen watching the painter paint a portrait of their daughter and her attendants (*las meniñas*). What Foucault notes, however, is that whoever looks at the painting is actually opposite the mirror and hence stands in "the place of the king."[1] Following Heidegger, the modern technological age can be seen as the era in which humans qua humans became the focal point for our understanding of the world, taking the place held in earlier eras by kings and gods. From this viewpoint, one way of understanding the postmodern would be as a way of thinking that puts human mastery of the world into question.

Another aspect of this text worth noting underscores how Foucault's work moves beyond the "humanism" found in Sartre's existentialism that marks it, for Heidegger, as still steeped in modernity. In the "Foreword to the English edition" [*sic*], Foucault makes a considerable effort to distinguish the approach to the material he discusses in this book from one "which gives absolute priority to the observing subject, . . .which places its own point of view at the origin of all history . . ." (OT xiv). Foucault seeks to emphasize the extent to which the subject is shaped by the objects that he or she observes, especially in the human (i.e., social) sciences; the extent to which acts are imbedded, as Merleau-Ponty reminds us, in a largely implicit perceptual world; and the extent to which history is shaped by factors outside human control, and often human knowledge. The place of the king is no longer taken by "man," because the postmodern world is not a picture at which "man" gazes, but a network of interrelationships that exceed our grasp at every moment. There is no Being in Foucault, but there are beings, things that are ordered. As his thought progresses it becomes clearer that, for him, the development of "biopower" has already moved human existence squarely into the realm of a "standing reserve" that Heidegger attributes to things alone. We have already moved, that is, from being Subjects to being subjected (as Voldemort seeks to subject even his followers to his arbitrary power).

In his earlier work, Foucault makes this point by tracing detailed "archeologies" or "genealogies" of major institutions of modern European life: the medical clinic, the insane asylum, the prison. *The Order of Things* is somewhat different in that it traces the development of three intellectual fields of thought—philology, biology, and economics—from what he calls the "pre-classical" period to the forms they take in the nineteenth century. What he establishes, in brief, is that in each of these fields, the basic understanding of the subject matter—language, life, money—switches from a static array of variables in fixed time/space to a roughly evolutionary model seen, not from a "god's-eye view" as before, but from the perspective of how humans can intervene in and control its future development in ways that serve human purposes. The conclusion he draws echoes in different ways both Aristotle and Heidegger: "man is neither the oldest nor the most constant problem that has been posed for human knowledge. . . . As the archeology of our thought easily shows, man is an invention of recent date. And one perhaps nearing its end" (OT 386–387). In his later work, however, Foucault is concerned less with the end of the age of "man" (again, the gendered word his language provides) than with the ways in which "biopower" may perpetuate itself endlessly on human bodies.

II

It is in his work on the history of the prison, *Discipline and Punish* (1975), that Foucault most clearly begins to develop his concept of "biopower." He begins with the end of public executions accompanied by torture that were common up until about the time of the French and American revolutions, and traces two paradoxes in the changes that follow. First, he notes the elimination of "corporal punishment" (what the U.S. Constitution calls "cruel and unusual punishment"), but then is forced to consider "What would a non-corporal punishment be?" Second, he goes on to ask, "If the penalty in its most severe forms no longer addresses itself to the body, on what does it lay hold?" The surprising answer is, "since it is no longer the body, it must be the soul"[2] (which is, of course, literally true of the soul-sucking dementors who guard Azkaban, the prison in Harry Potter's world), this despite the secular orientation of the regimes (the U.S., post-Revolutionary France, etc.), under which the modern prison largely developed. Foucault notes also that he intends to place the history of the prison in the context of the history of the social sciences to find "some common matrix . . . ; in short, [to] make the technology of power the very principle both of the humanization of the penal system and of the knowledge of man" (DP 23). In part, this reflects Foucault's developing concept of "biopower," but it also reflects the increasing involvement over the period he studies social scientists and what we now call mental health professionals in the evolution of the prison.

Before the modern period, Foucault tells us, imprisonment was not in itself a form of punishment. Bodies were confined as a form of security in lieu of payment or as a substitute for penal servitude for those (women, children, the sick) incapable of it (DP 118). (Azkaban punishes as much by keeping inmates in constant close contact with the Dementors as by confining them.) Foucault traces parallels between the development of the prison and that of the "poor house," the military, and the school, and notes that "The historical moment of the disciplines was the moment when an art of the human body was born, which was directed not only at the growth of its skills, nor at the intensification of its subjection, but at the formation of a relation that in the mechanism itself makes it more obedient as it becomes more useful, and conversely." Military training is one example. It turns individuals into a bonded unit while it increases their abilities as individuals. Such disciplinary procedures "dissociates power from the body; on the one hand, it turns [the body's power] into an 'aptitude,' a 'capacity,' which it seeks to increase; on the other hand, it reverses the course of the energy, the power that might result from [this process], and turns it into a relation of strict subjection [of the individual to authority]" (DP 137–138). This is clearly an early description of how "biopower" works.

On another level, however, a major part of Foucault's point here is that all this doesn't happen as a result of explicit human intentions. "It is rather a multiplicity of often minor processes, of different origin and scattered location, which overlap, repeat, or imitate one another . . . converge and gradually produce the blueprint of a general method" (DP 138). As with the development of humans as part of the "standing reserve" in the age of technology for Heidegger, the power that is both created and exerted here is outside the sphere of human reason or control. And the goal of this impersonal process is not only power, but also knowledge. He says of the Walnut Street Prison in Philadelphia that became a model for much of the later development of the prison that "this control and transformation of behavior were accompanied—both as a condition and as a consequence—by the development of a knowledge of the individuals" so that "the prison functions as an apparatus of knowledge" (DP 125–126). Foucault then comes to a famous and, in my opinion, chilling conclusion: "We must cease once and for all to describe the effects of power in negative terms . . . In fact, power produces; it produces reality; it produces domains of subject and rituals of truth. The individual and the knowledge that may be gained of him belong to this production" (DP 194).

This conclusion leads Foucault to consider what he calls the "self-evidence" of the prison, its immediate acceptance by society once the concept was introduced at the beginning of the nineteenth century. "How could the prison not be immediately accepted when, by locking up, retraining and rendering docile, it merely reproduces, with a little more emphasis, all the mechanisms that are to be found in the social body?" (DP 233). That is, in his terms, the prison is central to a whole complex of institutions and mechanisms, including again the school and the military, "which all tend, like the prison, to exercise a power of normalization" that are "applied not to transgressions against a 'central' law, but to the apparatus of production . . . and to a whole multiplicity" of abnormalities presided over by "the rules of strategy" (DP 308). A few years later, he would talk about this configuration as a result of the convergence of state power and a "pastoral" power that originated in Christian institutions such as the monastery.[3] This is the source of the ability of prisons and similar governmental institutions to shape and control the "soul" by coming to know its individual truth. He concludes that "We have to promote new forms of subjectivity through the refusal of this kind of individuality which has been imposed on us for several centuries."[4]

III

The concept of "biopower" took full form in Foucault's *The History of Sexuality, Volume I: An Introduction* (1976). He begins there where he left off in *Discipline and Punish*, with the redefinition of power as productive rather than repressive, which results in his critique of the "repressive hypothesis," the claim that in the nineteenth-century sexuality was repressed. He asks whether the repressive hypothesis itself is not part of the same development of "biopower" as the repression it asserts. "The object," he tells us, "is to define the regime of power-knowledge-pleasure that sustains the discourse on human sexuality in our part of the world."[5] Here, again, he traces elements of this regime back to monastic practices of confession that "The seventeenth century made . . . a rule for everyone" (HS 20), and notes that the emergence of "population" as a major area of political concern was in reality a concern about reproduction and hence about sex (HS 25). The focus on population led to a focus on reproductive sex and generated a category of the "unnatural" and a political concern with it that had not existed before. "The sodomite had been a temporary aberration; the homosexual was now a species" (HS 43).

He associates this development with the way in which medical science at the time, "more servile with respect to the powers of order than amenable to the requirements of truth" established "an entire pornography of the morbid" in the late nineteenth century based on a confessional discourse about sex (HS 54). Rather than seeing this confessional discourse as freeing, he sets it in the context of the historical development of technology that Heidegger describes, and considers this process part of "An immense labor to which the West has submitted generations in order to produce . . . men's subjection," which he equates with "their constitution as subjects in both senses of the word" (HS 60). This "confessional science" (HS 64) also operated, as did the prison, as a form of normalization: "the sexual domain . . . was placed under the rule of the normal and the pathological" (HS 67). A major assumption of his method in exploring this history, however, is that "there is no power that is exercised without a series of aims and objectives. But this does not mean that it results from the choice or decision of an individual subject" (HS 95). This is why, in response to the legal, psychiatric, and other discourses that created "the homosexual," there arose a counterdiscourse that asserted the "legitimacy or 'naturality'" of homosexuality, "often in the same vocabulary" (HS 101).

But "the homosexual" was not the first, or the primary, target of the explosion of confessional discourse about sex. The concern with population guaranteed that "one of the first to be 'sexualized' was the 'idle' woman," the middle-class wife (HS 121). This was because the initial focus was on "the body, vigor, longevity, progeniture, and descent of the classes that 'ruled,'" so that this new "political ordering of life" was created "not through an enslavement of others, but through an affirmation of self" (HS 123). This meant that the discourse of sexuality "induces specific class effects" (HS 127), as in the connections both Lucius and Draco Malfoy consistently make between the number of the Weasley's children and their financial problems. We see in these gender dynamics a form of "logic" that will become generalized in Derrida (also specifically with regard to the situation of women). Foucault notes that "'sex' was defined in three ways: as that which belongs in common to men and women; as that which belongs, *par excellence*, to men, and hence is lacking in women; but at the same time, as that which by itself constitutes woman's body . . ." (HS 153). That is, all humans have a sexuality, but locating sexuality in male reproductive anatomy left literally no place for female sexuality, while at the same time sexuality became the essence of female existence, since everything else about women was judged in terms of its relationship to their sexuality.

Foucault's response to the central role of sexuality in the development of "biopower" is that "The rallying point for the counterattack against the deployment of sexuality ought not to be sex-desire, but bodies and pleasures" (HS 157). He believes that "we need a new economy of power relations" for reasons that echo ontological humility. He believe normalization moves closer to understanding human existence as "standing reserve" because, "The relationship between rationalization [of governmental/managerial processes] and excesses of political power is evident." For him, the best approach is to "analyze specific rationalities" and to oppose, not power per se, but the "power effect" or "a technique, a form of power" (MF 210–212). Behind this apparent ontological humility, however, lies a very strong claim to knowledge, to a univocal interpretation of the history of the modern world. This view assumes both that this history is a single one, uniform across the West (so France can serve as both model and exemplar of it) and that the historical processes under discussion are still produced at the human level, even if outside the scope of explicit human intention and knowledge.

Against this one could argue, for instance, that any claims about a "racism against the abnormal"[6] ought to take the particular history of the interaction between racism and slavery in the United States directly into account, rather than subsuming it under the case of France, especially given the worldwide penetration of that specific history in the last century through the dominance of American popular culture. Similarly, in discussing the history of sexuality, it seems strange to cite and then largely ignore the gendered differences in that history that create widely divergent lived experiences of male, female, and intersex bodies.[7] Moreover, for Foucault there are impersonal forces at work here, but they never transcend the human; one suspects that, for him, they cannot because nothing does. So his solutions are human solutions, local revolts at the edges of modernity that offer no clear vision of what a better, different future might be, nor any guide for getting from here to there.

Foucault's genealogical method has considerable value in revealing the need for ontological humility, as we will see in the next chapter. At the same time, however, there is a profound paradox in the production of what is supposed to be the "truth" about the history of the West by someone who believes that "truth is not by nature free . . . its production is thoroughly imbued with relations of power" (HS 60). In fact, Foucault decenters "man" only in favor of the impersonal effects of human actions and, as in Spinoza, does so only on the basis of a claim to absolute knowledge, compounded by an absolute denial of transcendence. Just as he may have seen himself as recommending a sort of localized guerrilla warfare against "biopower" from its edges, he can also be seen as attacking the modern technological age only at its edges, on those points where its power is already on the wane, and leaving unchallenged those aspects most directly opposed to the ontological humility needed to prevent the complete reduction of human bodies and human lives to "standing reserve."[8]

Derrida: Linguistic Humility

> [T]he subject . . . is inscribed in language, is a "function" of language, becomes a *speaking* subject only by making its speech conform—even in so-called "creation," or in so-called "transgression"—to the system of the rules of languages as a system of differences . . .
>
> —Jacques Derrida, "Différance"

I

We have already seen the importance of language in Merleau-Ponty's later work and the importance of discourse in Foucault. For Derrida, language is at the center of the postmodern undermining of the primacy of the Cartesian Subject. He is also fully aware, however, of the paradoxes of his own situation, which generates a level of complexity in his thought that is unusual even in philosophy: he questions the meaning of a signature and then signs his work;[9] he writes double texts parallel to each other side by side on the page (*Glas*[10]), or as text and footnote ("Living On: *Border Lines*"[11]), or puts his text side by side with a prolonged quotation (M x–xxix); he even writes in letters and post cards (*The Post Card*[12]). Underneath all this literal play of language, though, is a profound awareness of to what extent language shapes our thought.

No stronger proof of this can be found than the word "différance," which is central to this aspect of Derrida's thought and yet makes even less sense in English than in French. In French the verb *différer* combines the English verbs to differ and to defer; the French *différence* (with an "e") refers, as does the English, only to differing. This allows Derrida to create the word différance (with an "a"), to refer to both senses of the French verb at once. Moreover, he notes that "the ending -*ance* remains undecided *between* the active and the passive" (M 9, his emphasis). He argues that différance is the primary dynamic of language, which works as a system of differences and deferrals. According to structural linguistics, on one level, language is based on the differences between sounds: *mmm-aaa* is the largest such difference, and hence the easiest for babies to learn; conversely, in Spanish *d* is pronounced as a sound between the hard English *d* and *t* that many English speakers cannot hear because the difference is too small. That is, in language as in music we don't first hear sounds, we hear the differences between sounds, the acoustic and temporal spaces between them.

On another level, as suggested with regard to Merleau-Ponty, structural linguistics argues that the meaning of a word depends on where it fits in a system of differences between words, so that a chair is a piece of furniture that is not a stool, or a bench, or a throne, and so on. This means that "every concept is inscribed in a chain or in a system within which it refers to other, to other concepts, by means of the systematic play of differences." So words never refer simply to an object or idea, but always carry the echo of all the things that whatever they refer to might be but is not (M 11–13). On yet another level, the word is generally understood to be a sign that "takes the place of the present [thing]" that it refers to in its absence and so is the "deferred presence" of that thing (M 9). In any case, the final meaning of the word is always deferred (in time) and based on a system of differences (in space). This is why différance is "literally neither a word nor a concept" (M 3), because it names the process of differing in space and deferring over time that makes both words and concepts possible.

In the article "Différance," Derrida also takes care to describe the relationship between his work and Heidegger's discussions of time and space in *Being and Time* as "a strict communication, even though not an exhaustive and irreducibly necessary one" (M 10). Clearly he shares many of Heidegger's concerns about the modern technological age. He echoes, for instance, elements of Heidegger's argument in "The Letter on Humanism," saying that structural linguistics (as well as the work of Nietzsche, Sigmund Freud, and others) imply that we must take consciousness "no longer as the absolutely central form of Being but as a 'determination' and as an 'effect'. . . of *différance*" (M 16). One can see how this decentering happens most clearly in Freud because différance names the two things an infant must learn in order to become a conscious self: that he or she is separated or different from his or her mother (as opposed to the prenatal state) and that he or she must delay or defer gratification (e.g., by waiting to be fed). We start out life as an inchoate bundle of organic needs and only later become the consciousness with which Descartes, Sartre, and so on, begin philosophy (M 18).

Derrida, however, differentiates his work from Heidegger's in several ways. Most notably, perhaps, in place of Heidegger's attempt to go beyond, or behind, the metaphysical tradition that results in our modern world, Derrida insists that "For us, *différance* remains a metaphysical name" because he sees no clear or easy way to evade metaphysics. He is also suspicious of possible narrowly religious interpretations of Heidegger. "This unnameable is not an ineffable Being which no name could approach: God, for example." Instead, he notes that one effect of différance is that "There will be no unique name, even if it were the name of Being." (Perhaps there is a distant echo, or denial, of this in the use of He-who-must-not-be-named to refer to Voldemort in the Harry Potter stories.) For Derrida, the ubiquitous play of différance puts into question both "nostalgia" for "a lost native country of thought" (perhaps Heidegger's ancient Greece) and "what I will call Heideggerian *hope*" (M 26–27, his emphasis), and in so doing raises both skepticism and ontological humility to levels not seen in the philosophy at least since Hume.

II

The book that brought Derrida the same notoriety in the United States that *The History of Sexuality* brought Foucault was *Of Grammatology*, which was originally written at roughly the same time as "Différance," although not published in English until 1976. In "Différance," one can see one of the main themes, if they can be called that, of the longer work: "There is no purely and rigorously phonetic writing. So-called phonetic writing . . . can function only by admitting into its system nonphonetic 'signs' (punctuation, spacing, etc.)" (M 5)—whence the title *Margins*. *Of Grammatology* and other works written around the same time are extended studies of why the European tradition has historically privileged the spoken word over the written word and how that privilege can be "deconstructed" (a term we'll define after we've seen how it works in specific cases) in several of the key texts of that tradition. We see an echo of this preference for the spoken word in Harry Potter's world, where the Marauder's Map is almost the only positive example of written magic (and Tom Riddle's diary provides a warning against the dangers of the written word when "you can't tell where it keeps its brain"[13]). Even witches and wizards share our tradition's prejudice in favor of the (sometimes silent) spoken word.

In *Of Grammatology*, Derrida characterizes the traditional, prestructuralist view of language: "The formal essence of the signified is *presence*, and the privilege of its proximity to the logos [word] as *phonè* [sound] is the privilege of presence."[14] "Presence" is another key term in Derrida's work, with links to Heidegger's "present-at-hand," the secondary and "privative" way in which beings (and ultimately Dasein) are understood in the modern age. We already saw that, on the traditional account, the word, or signifier, stands in for the absent object, or signified, which would otherwise, and ideally, be present itself. The word is "close to," but not quite the thing itself, and the "closer" it is the better the word does its job as, for example, the "armchair" is "closer" to the thing itself than the bare word "chair." Sound comes into it for the very simple reason that when we hear ourselves speak there seems to be no difference between the speaking subject and the subject who hears. This creates the illusion that the spoken word is interior to consciousness itself and only becomes external to it when written down. The spoken word appears to be immediately (literally, without mediation) present to us, and so is given a privileged relationship with consciousness. As already noted, however, this is wrong. Sound *is* a medium as external to consciousness as writing. American sign language is as much "speech" to its users as the spoken word is to the hearing.

Thus, Derrida's strong claim: "If 'writing' signifies inscription . . . , writing in general covers the entire field of linguistic signs" (OG 44). This is because all signs exist as physical entities outside the consciousness, and control, of the speaking subject since they are part of, and governed by, the system of physical signs that make up a language. "From the moment there is meaning, there is nothing but signs" (OG 50), because meaning is the relationship between the sign and what it represents. At the same time, structural linguistics has shown that it is impossible that "a sign, the unity of a signifier and a signified, be produced within the plenitude of a present and absolute presence," because, as we have seen, the sign always also refers to the place of that sign in the system as a whole (OG 69). The term "piano stool," used to refer to what is in reality usually a small bench, for instance, drags in its wake, as it were, the entire history of piano-related furniture, no matter what a particular speaker or writer might intend by using it. This linguistic "baggage" is, in part, what creates the possibility of intentional transgressions, such as the modified chair used by the eccentric pianist Glenn Gould. Because the linguistic system "goes far beyond the possibilities of the 'intentional consciousness'" of whoever might use the sign, it also both "constitutes and effaces so-called conscious subjectivity . . ." (OG 84).

Among the many other points that Derrida makes in this book is that the claim that European languages use strictly phonetic writing, in addition to being illusory, carries an implicit value judgment in its own favor, so that nonphonetic systems of writing, such as Chinese ideographs, are seen as more primitive (like Egyptian hieroglyphs) and inferior. Instead, he argues that "'Phonetic' and 'nonphonetic' are therefore never pure qualities of certain systems of writing, they are the abstract characteristics of typical elements, more or less numerous and dominant within all systems of signification in general" (OG 89). What is of interest here is less the claim itself than the form of his argument, which is repeated throughout his work. He calls it the "double gesture" in which, on the one hand, the tradition identifies one aspect of its manifestation and claims to possess it in an (impossible) pure form (consciousness, the spoken word, phonetic writing) as a simple descriptive fact while, on the other hand, making an implicit value judgment against its opposite (the nonconscious, the mediated word, nonphonetic writing) *and* against those persons, cultures, and so forth, identified with that opposite (mental illness, the written word [but also American sign language], the Chinese language, etc.).

This provides a clear example of "deconstruction," the way of reading texts for which Derrida is best known (although, like much else is Derrida, it has its roots in Heidegger's thought). Deconstruction as a critical method is also a double gesture. The first step is to identifies a key concept in a text and locate it as part of a lengthy list of interrelated hierarchical dualisms:

God	man
good	evil
rational	irrational
form	matter
life	death
human	Nature
mind	body
male	female
⋮	⋮
the spoken word	the written word
phonetic writing	non-phonetic writing

(Note the overlap here with the list in chapter 2 that grows out of Heidegger's later work, as well as the isomorphism of the dualism male/female with the others Derrida would undermine.).

As Derrida explains with regard to the case of the written word in *Of Grammatology*, "writing, the letter, the sensible inscription, has always been considered by Western tradition as the body and matter external to the spirit, to breath, to speech and to the logos. And the problem of soul and body is no doubt derived from the problem of writing from which it seems, conversely to borrow its metaphors" (OG 35). Besides situating the concept in these hierarchical dualisms, he also underscores the value judgments inherent in that move, no matter what the conscious intention of those who use that concept. To call a male a "girl," or a slang equivalent, can be an unconscious gesture, but it is always one that maintains and reinforces the oppression of women.

In a second gesture, Derrida then shows how a text can be "deconstructed" along the "fault line" created by these dualisms to reveal the paradoxes and other signs of internal incoherence that are caused by its reliance on one or more of them. All texts can be deconstructed in this way, even Derrida's, because of the play of différance, which makes these dualisms inherently and necessarily unstable. His work, therefore, is largely critical, focused not on finding some other, better truth, but on revealing the structures that lie at the core of the central texts of the European tradition.

III

Given the compounded complexity of their texts, it should not be surprising that Derrida's deconstructions of Heidegger are especially torturous, as indicated by the title "*Ousia* and *Grammē*: Note on a Note from *Being and Time*." As the two primary sources of the concept of ontological humility, however, it makes some sense to try to see their thought in a common perspective, even if only in brief outline. Adding Aristotle into the mix will not make it easier to gain clarity here, but will narrow the focus of the comparison to one text and one relatively limited set of topics, "the vulgar" (Heidegger's term) concept of time as a real element of the physical world (as reflected in Hermione's Time-Turner in *Harry Potter and the Prisoner of Azkaban*) and the essence (*ousia*) of beings as presence in the present moment. It is also not inconsequential for Derrida that this discussion occurs in a footnote, "by far the longest," almost at the very end of *Being and Time* (M 35).

Derrida begins by noting the point of departure that he could be said to share with Heidegger, the belief that "From Parmenides to Husserl, the privilege of the present has never been put into question. It could not have been. It is what is self-evident itself, and no thought seems possible outside of its element. Nonpresence is always thought in the form of presence . . . or as a modalization of presence" (M 34). Aristotle, Derrida tells us, tries to think time in terms of the present moment, the "now," and discovers this now doesn't exist, since it is "that which is *no longer* and as that which is *not yet*." Conversely, time can also be understood as the becoming past of the present, so that the now (because it is [fixed] and not in process) falls outside of time as "an intemporal kernel of time." Derrida further explains this by saying that "in order to be a being [the now] must not be affected by time," because "[b]eings are what *is*" (M 39–40, his emphasis). Thus, Heidegger reveals why metaphysics believed "it could think time on the basis of a being already silently predetermined in its relation to time" and, to this extent, *Being and Time* "constitutes a decisive step beyond *or within* metaphysics" (M 47, my emphasis).

Derrida notes, however, that by effectively denying that time exists, Aristotle sees it in the same way as Kant and Heidegger, "as the condition for the possibility of the appearance of beings." Thus, "What Aristotle has set down, then, is both the traditional metaphysical security [in the simple presence of the present moment] and, in its inaugural ambiguity, the critique of this security." Derrida questions whether Heidegger has fully understood this (M 48–49), and then moves from the two ways of understanding the now (as the presence of the present and as outside of time) to say that "The *meaning* of time is thought on the basis of the present as nontime. And this could not be otherwise. . . . The concept of . . . meaning, is governed by the entire system of determinations that we are pointing out here, and every time that a question of *meaning* is posed, it must be posed within the closure of metaphysics" (M 51–52, his emphasis).For Derrida, this would include Heidegger's question of the meaning of Being. He concludes that "every text of metaphysics carries within itself . . . *both* the so-called 'vulgar' concept of time [as a series of nows] *and* the resources that will be borrowed from the system of metaphysics in order to criticize that concept," and again raises the question of what would be "the conditions for a discourse exceeding metaphysic" as Heidegger purports to do (M 60–61, his emphasis).

From all this, Derrida draws three conclusions. The first is "That perhaps there is no 'vulgar concept of time.' The concept of time . . . belongs to metaphysics, and it names the domination of presence." In applying this to *Being and Time* he also investigates some of the other dualisms Heidegger seems to rely on there (including the pair primordial/privative that operates in the discussion of the present-at-hand), but his second conclusion is one that he never steps away from: "That the question we are [here] asking remains within Heidegger's thought" (M 63–64). Finally, he questions whether the respect for the difference between Being and beings (and Dasein) that figures so prominently in Heidegger's reading of the ancient Greeks can actually be understood as being about an ancient thought to which we have, after all, only extremely limited access, or whether it must be seen as Heidegger through and through. He refers to "The relationship between the two texts [Aristotle's and Heidegger's], between presence in general . . . and that which exceeds it before or beyond Greece—such a relationship can never offer itself in order to be read in the form of presence, supposing that anything can ever offer itself in order to be *read* in such a form" (M 65, his emphasis). That is, even if a text could offer itself in this straightforward a way, the relationship between Heidegger's work and the ancient Greeks could not, because the latter is forever lost in time.

Derrida: Humility Unto Death

> One simply keeps on denying the aporia and antimony [of moral responsibility], tirelessly, and one treats as nihilist, relativist, even poststructuralist, and worse still deconstructionist, all those who remain concerned in the face of such a display of good conscience.
>
> —Jacques Derrida, *The Gift of Death*

I

The thread in Derrida's work that focuses on death and responsibility, like Heidegger's simultaneous readings of the ancient Greeks and his critique of modernity, doesn't keep the focus on language that is most prominent in his earlier work, but rather grows out of it to become a major theme in Derrida's later work. Already in "Différance," he notes that the *a* in this word "remains silent, secret and discreet as a tomb" (M 4). Some of his other early articles, especially those that focus on Freud, continue the theme of death in his deconstructions. Freud also provides the bridge between the theme of death and another theme that emerges in Derrida's work, the deconstruction of gender and of oppression in general. There is no simple way to explain the link between death and the feminine in Freud, but one way to think about it would be that, biologically speaking, once a woman is impregnated, the male's role in the reproduction of the species is complete and even his death won't interfere with the reproductive goal of sex (e.g., the praying mantis). Another way would be to consider the traditional role of women as the keepers of tombs and graves (e.g., the story of the Resurrection or Freud's favorite, Sophocles's Oedipus plays). In the contemporary world, moreover, women outlive men more often than the reverse, another way in which women can be linked to death in a culture dominated by a male point of view. This symbolism is so natural that it is a woman, a blood relative, who kills Sirius Black.

A more subtle and more detailed example of this association between women and death can be found in *Memoirs of the Blind*, a book Derrida wrote to accompany an exhibition at the Louvre held in 1990–91. At the end of this book, he asks (in parentheses), "for if there are many great blind men, why so many weeping women?"[15] At the beginning of the same text, he had already noted that "the illustrious blind of our culture are almost always men, 'the great blind men,' as if women perhaps saw to it never to risk their sight." In a footnote to this comment, he suggests that one reason for this gender bias with regard to blindness might be the fact that "These narratives are dominated by the filiation father/son that we will see haunting so many drawings" (MB 5–6). Blindness is linked to death in this text in many ways, for instance, by one of the full-page reproductions that accompany it, which tells the story of the blessing of Jacob by the blind and dying Isaac (MB 22, detail 99), and several drawings of the dead or dying with their eyes closed, including a self-portrait by Gustave Courbet (MB 78–81). These hints, and others scattered through the text, suggest that the same cultural artifacts that associate the masculine with blindness also casts the feminine (out) in the role of grieving survivors.

In *The Gift of Death* (1992), which focuses on the work of Czech philosopher Jan Patočka (who died in police custody), Derrida notes that in *Being and Time* death serves both as one way that we discover Angst and as what individuate us. This second claim is based on Heidegger's belief that "The nullity by which Dasein's Being is dominated primordially through and through, is revealed to Dasein itself in authentic Being-towards-death" (BT 354). That is, when Dasein authentically knows it will die, it also comes to understand the randomness and contingency of its existence, and how it is mired in its social (and linguistic) world. Living in full awareness of death is how one lives an authentic life, another theme from Rowling's saga. For Derrida, this means, "The identity of the oneself is *given* by death, by the being-towards-death," because only I can die *my* death. Derrida also says that "in none of these discourses we are analyzing here does the moment of death give room for one to take into account sexual difference; as if, as it would be tempting to imagine, sexual difference does not count in the fact of death. Sexual difference would be a being-*up-until* death."[16] That is, death is represented as gender-neutral. Given the history of claims to gender neutrality in the tradition, however, this means, again, that death will always be male. In the discussion of Kierkegaard that follows, however, Derrida counters this tradition by referring to the knight of faith as "she" (D 63).

Through Kierkegaard's "Fear and Trembling," Derrida returns to Isaac, but the young Isaac whose father, Abraham, was willing to offer him as a sacrifice. "The reading, interpretation, and tradition of the sacrifice of Isaac are themselves sites of bloody, holocaustic, sacrifice. Isaac's sacrifice continues every day" (presumably in the Arab–Israeli conflict, GD 70). Referring to the "double gesture" in the title of his book—death as a gift, the gift given by death—he asks, as in *Memoirs of the Blind*, "Does the system of this sacrificial responsibility and of the double 'gift of death' imply at its very basis an exclusion or sacrifice of woman?" He also notes, however, that "In the case of the tragic hero or the tragic sacrifice [as opposed to Abraham's religious sacrifice of Isaac in Kierkegaard], woman is present, her place is central" (after all, Harry's mother dies to protect him, too). Derrida then repeats Beauvoir's warning that there may be more than one Other to whom we have a moral duty. "Everything points to the fact that one is unable to be responsible at the same time before the other and before others, before the others of the other." Abraham can fully honor God, in Kierkegaard, only by going beyond the Universal that would allow him to explain his action to those around him (most notably Sarah), so he necessarily fails to honor his ethical duty to them. There can be no justification or good conscience: "a decision is, in the end, always secret" (GD 76–77).

II

Derrida's increasingly explicit interest in politics in his later work takes a clear form in *The Politics of Friendship* (1994). He uses an ambiguous and cryptic quotation he attributes to Aristotle—"Oh, my friends, there is no friend"—as a starting place for a reconsideration of the possibility of democracy, since Aristotle himself describes friendship as the basis of the political state.[17] Derrida devotes much of this book to discussing the relationship between friendship and brotherhood, a political concept in France, where "fraternity" comes after only liberty and equality as a public virtue. He comments several times on the gender bias of this virtue, what he calls the "androcentric" structure of friendship.[18] He also notes that the supposed line from Aristotle could also be (and usually is) translated as "too many friends means no friends," which "reopens the question of multiplicity, the question of the one and of the 'more than one,'" that is, the issue of our duties to multiple others (including, he emphasizes, feminine others—the French word for "the other" [*l'autre*] has no visible or audible gender, but is grammatically masculine). This second translation of Aristotle also refers us indirectly back to the *a* in différance, since "it all comes down to less than a letter, to the difference of breathing" (the translations rely on different ways of accenting the letter omega in the Greek text, PF 209).

One of Derrida's goals in *The Politics of Friendship* text is to *"think an alterity without hierarchical difference at the root of democracy,"* which he believes would "free a certain interpretation of *equality* by removing it from the . . . schema of *fraternity*" (PF 232, his emphasis). He has already argued that brotherhood, and by extension friendship, gain much of their strength from the exclusion of the nonbrother/friend, that is, first of all, the sister, but also the unrelated other, the stranger, the foreigner, and the immigrant (a pattern we will see again in the next chapter). A democracy based on brotherhood is one based on the same series of hierarchical dualisms that are the linchpin of a deconstructive analysis. True political equality would break the historical connection between democracy and hierarchy, not by making "all men [*sic*] brothers," but by freeing the political state from the control of this dualism, and perhaps moving it beyond hierarchical dualisms altogether. "Is this incommensurable friendship, this friendship of the incommensurable, indeed the one we are here attempting to separate from its fraternal adherence . . . ? Or is it still a fraternity, but a fraternity divided in its concept, a fraternity ranging infinitely beyond all literal figures of the brother, a fraternity that would no longer exclude anyone?" Put differently, is the relative equality of women in Harry Potter's world enough, if it ends in a society that excludes and persecutes muggles and "mudbloods"?

Derrida's answer to this question is to say, "Here we encounter the gravest of problems" because "it is not our intention to denounce fraternity." Still, the play of différance means that a word's meaning exceeds the realm of human intentions. "In keeping this word to designate a fraternity beyond fraternity . . . one never renounces that which one claims to renounce—and which returns in myriad ways, through symptoms and disavowals whose rhetoric we must learn to decipher and whose strategy to outwit" (PF 237). Thus, he refers again to "the *double exclusion* we see at work in all the great ethico-politico-philosophical discourses on friendship: on the one hand, the exclusion of friendship between women; on the other the exclusion of friendship between a man and a women" (PF 278–279, his emphasis). From there he moves to terrain that is a commonplace of contemporary feminism:

> The *double exclusion* of the feminine would not be unrelated to the movement that has always 'politicized' the friendship model at the very moment when one strives to rescue it from thoroughgoing politicization. The tension here is on the side of the political itself. It is at work in all the discourses that reserve politics and public space to man, domestic and private space to woman. (PF 281)

Derrida, however, clearly sets this commonplace in a context that links it to the general discourse of political exclusion.

III

In *Of Hospitality* (1997), another of his dual texts written across the page from a text by Anne Dufourmantelle, Derrida investigates the ethico-politico-philosophical question of the foreigner and the immigrant in more detail, but interlinked with the question of the women and the problem of language, now a concrete as well as a theoretical issue. He says, "That is where the question of hospitality begins: must we ask the foreigner to understand us, to speak our language . . . before being able and so as to be able to welcome him into our country?"[19] Hospitality is, he notes, always a commitment on the part of a household, of a family (OH 23). He suggests that the question of the foreigner can be seen as "the question of the question"—"Does hospitality consist in interrogating the new arrival?" or "does hospitality begin with the unquestioning welcome" (OH 28–29). More generally, he cites "the constant collusion between traditional hospitality, hospitality in the ordinary sense, and power." Power comes into the equation because of "the necessity, for the host, for the one who receives, of choosing, electing, filtering, selecting their invitees, visitors, or guests. . . . No hospitality without sovereignty of oneself over one's home . . ." (OH 55). Here the hierarchical dualism of public/private enters the picture as well, and with it the issue of gender and family.[20]

This is because "Usually, the foreigner . . . is defined on the basis of birth." Himself an Algerian-born French citizen (since birth) who lived in France, Derrida uses the postwar term "displaced persons" as well as "exiles, those who are deported, expelled, rootless, nomads" to name those who "share two sources of sighs, two nostalgias: their dead ones [whose graves they cannot visit] and their languages" (OH 87). Yet he considers "the mother tongue" a "*fantasy*" of something that would be truly one's own, even in exile or displacement, because it never entirely belongs to anyone because of the play of différance (OH 89). As is clear in the contemporary debate in the United States about "English only" legislation, the idea of a "mother tongue" links the sovereignty that gives one the power to extend or deny hospitality with what we learned earlier about the illusory closeness of the spoken word to consciousness. Derrida says that "Is there hospitality without at least the fantasy of this auto-nomy [the Greek roots of this word suggests both self-governing and self-naming]? Of this . . . auto-affection of which hearing-oneself-speak is the privileged figure?" (OH 137). Language, spoken language, always seems closest to us, and so most our own. To speak another's language is always, therefore, alienating, if only because "Speaking the same language is not only a linguistic operation. It's a matter of *ethos* [a way of living] generally" (OH 133). The alien is therefore alien not only to those whose hospitality he or she seeks, but to him- or herself.

Hospitality is ultimately impossible for Derrida, on one level because it must be unconditional (the failing of the Dursleys, Harry's foster family), but unconditional hospitality puts the domestic others to whom the host also has duties at risk (his Biblical examples are both graphic and extreme). On another level, hospitality assumes a sovereignty that is undermined by the system of hierarchical dualisms. In this way it belongs to a long list of ethico-politico-philosophical "impossibles" with which Derrida concerns himself in his last works, including the gift (which must be given without expectation of a gift in return, but could not exist as a gift outside a system of such reciprocal giving) and forgiveness ("*one only forgives the unforgiveable*").[21] On a smaller scale, he considers "the intellectual" ("most often masculine gender," PM 34) as another "impossible" because, on the one hand, of the need to combat the "anti-intellectual" while acknowledging, on the other hand, that "an agreed definition of 'the intellectual' seems . . . more and more debatable . . ." In that context, he describes the impossibility of all these impossibles as a vision of a life "with no established *criteria*, with no given *rules* for knowledge or determinant judgment, with no assurance, . . . according to the 'dangerous perhaps' that Nietzsche talks about." A life that is "a form of endurance that is necessary *as such*" (PM 38, his emphasis).

In these later article, he touches on many themes central to ontological humility. One is the "transcendental," a metaphysical term that seems incongruous with Derrida's rejection of the metaphysical being suggested here. Again, he sees his use of the term as a double gesture that is ultimately "A question of problematic context and strategies," as with the term *intellectual*: "one must *in this place* relentlessly affirm questions of the transcendental type; and *in that place*, almost simultaneously, also ask questions about the history and the limits of what is called 'transcendental'" (PM 83). Similarly, he says, "I wouldn't reject the word *grace* . . . provided that it is not associated with obscure religious connotations . . ." (PM 132). Despite the lack of explicit political engagement in much of his early work, he also suggests a deep connection between the political and the philosophical that we will see in the next chapter as well: " 'True' political action always engages a philosophy. Every action and every political decision ought to invent their own norms or rules. Doing that goes through or implies philosophy" (PM

127). The equation he has been using, ethico-politico-philosophical, turns out to be a descriptive term that, perhaps ironically, has its roots in the same ancient Greek texts that fascinated Heidegger.

Death, however, is not only the ultimate "impossible" for Derrida, but also the best clue to his ontological humility. He says, "the possibility and immanence of death is not only a personal obsession, it's a way of surrendering to the necessity of what is given for thinking, namely that there is no presence without a trace [of what is not present] and no trace without [the possibility of the] disappearance of the origin of the said trace, thus no trace without [the hint of the] death [of its source]" (PM 158). As in Heidegger, my death is what is most uniquely my own, but can never, for me, be present. (We know, or can know, Harry Potter isn't dead when he has his last conversation with Dumbledore precisely because he is aware of himself having it.) Perhaps the governing hierarchical dualism for both Derrida and Heidegger is not, as fig. 4.1 on page 100 says, God/man, but life/death. If my death is never present for me, that dualism must collapse. And once one sees the impossibility of any absolute dualism, or any absolute hierarchy, both deconstruction as a method and ontological humility as a way of living seem to follow. As Derrida says, "faced with the infiniteness of responsibility, one can only admit to modesty, if not defeat. One is never equal to a responsibility that is assigned to us even before we have accepted it" (PM 139). From the moment, perhaps, as for Harry Potter, of our parents' deaths.

Chapter Five

Feminist Humility

Epistemologies of Ignorance[1]

> Epistemological choices about who to trust, what to believe, and why something is true are not benign academic issues. Instead, these concerns tap the fundamental question of which version of truth will prevail and shape thought and action.
>
> —Patricia Hill Collins, *Black Feminist Thought*

I

In this chapter, we will see how the ontological humility we saw earlier in Frye's work plays itself out in more recent feminist thought. We will first look at a thread of contemporary work in epistemology and science studies that focuses on so-called epistemologies of ignorance, and compare it with the earlier discussion of Heidegger's work. Then we will consider feminist theorist Patricia Hill Collins's work on the relationship between race and gender (which, as we saw, are explicit themes in Rowling's saga) and philosopher Ladelle McWhorter's account of the shared history of race and homophobia in the United States. In these texts, ontological humility remains a significant, if tacit, element in moving toward constructive solutions for the problems created in the modern world by the arrogance of those certain of the Truth of what they know.

The exact definition of "epistemologies of ignorance" is to some extent part of what is at issue in this section, but we can provisionally rely on the definition Nancy Tuana offers in her contribution to the volume of *Hypatia* devoted to that topic.[2] There she summarizes her argument for the importance of epistemologies of ignorance by pointing out that "if we are to fully understand the complex practices of knowledge production and the variety of factors that account for why something is known, we must also understand the practices that account for *not* knowing, that is, for our *lack* of knowledge about a phenomenon (SI 2)." In the same article, Tuana offers a typology of ways of "not knowing." The first three types, developed largely in the context of women's health issues, are fairly self-explanatory: (1) "knowing that we do not know, but not caring to know" (e.g., male contraceptives, SI 4); (2) what "we do not even know that we do not know" (e.g., the physiology of the clitoris, SI 6); and (3) what "they do not want us to know" (e.g., the dangers of oral contraceptives, SI 9–10). The fourth type Tuana calls "willful ignorance," which she defines as "an active ignoring of the oppression of others and one's role in that oppression" (SI 10–11). Much of the work in this area with regard to race has been done by Charles Mills, whose work we will discuss later.

The last two of Tuana's types require a bit more explanation. The first of these is "ignorance produced by the construction of epistemically disadvantaged identities." By this Tuana means to point to the fact that "our theories of knowledge and knowledge practices are far from democratic, maintaining criteria of credibility that favor members of privileged groups" (SI, 13). The classic example of this is Freud's refusal to believe his female patients when they reported incestuous advances by their fathers, but the Harry Potter saga abounds with examples of the ignorance of Voldemort and others that grows out of their refusal to pay any credence to what is said and done by "inferior" magical beings such as house-elves, goblins, and, perhaps more notably, children. Dumbledore say, "That which Voldemort does not value, he takes no trouble to comprehend."[3] This kind of ignorance has an internal link to "willful ignorance," since one way we can remain ignorant about oppression and our role in it is by discrediting or disallowing the testimony of those we oppress about their situation, as Mills also notes.

The last of Tuana's "types" of epistemology of ignorance she calls "loving ignorance," by which she means "ignorance of what exceeds our knowledge capacities," but Tuana calls it "loving," with a reference to Frye's account of "the loving eye" in the article discussed in the Prologue. Subsequent work by feminists of color such as María Lugones, in turn, uses the term in the specific context of the interaction between white feminists and feminists of color, where Tuana says it names "the realization that although much experience can be shared there will always be experiences that cannot" (SI 15–16). Cynthia Townley develops this theme in her contribution to the *Hypatia* volume, citing a controversial case from Australia in which a white feminist anthropologist was challenged by indigenous women over an article on rape in the indigenous community that had a single woman from one indigenous community as coauthor.[4] Although the above discussion of "epistemically disadvantaged identities" would apply to this example, here we will take the conversation in another direction.

Our starting point will be the fact that, unlike the others in Tuana's taxonomy, "loving ignorance" is a necessary form of ignorance; in her terms, it is "accepting what we cannot know" because the relevant realms of experience aren't available to us due to where we are socially situated with regard to our race, class, gender, sexuality, and so on (SI 15). For this reason, it requires a different analysis from those forms of ignorance that can be removed by efforts of epistemological and political will. There might be a justified reluctance to accept the idea that knowledge of the life experience of those unlike ourselves in socially important ways constitutes a necessary kind of ignorance, if the claim relied on assumptions about privileged access to the interiority of an atomic Cartesian self—but clearly that is not what Tuana means. Her discussion focuses rather on knowledge that comes from life experiences dependent on social locations defined by background conditions that, like language, cannot be made fully explicit under any epistemic circumstances. I cannot walk a mile in another's shoes and, if our starting points are far enough apart in sociopolitical space, any effort on my part to imaginatively put myself in her shoes without relying on her testimony as a primary source of information constitutes another form of arrogant ignorance. (This can be seen in Hermione's campaign on behalf of the house-elves at Hogwarts, whose lives she learns about from books without ever visiting the kitchen.)

Before moving on, it will be helpful to compare the work in epistemologies of ignorance done by Charles Mills with Tuana's account. In his contribution to *Race and Epistemologies of Ignorance*, Mills focuses on the racial dimension of "structural group-based miscognition."[5] He begins by rejecting the relativism that epistemologies of ignorance imply: "The phrase 'white ignorance' implies the possibility of a contrasting 'knowledge,' a contrast that would be lost if all claims to truth were equally spurious, or just a matter of competing discourses." He sees his own efforts in this area as a search for "genuine knowledge" (WI 15–16), and argues that in fact there is a knowledge about white ignorance in the black community that can be found in works of fiction, such as Ralph Ellison's *The Invisible Man*, but has rarely been addressed in the philosophical literature.

Mills looks in more detail at various ways in which white ignorance occurs and perpetuates itself, while acknowledging that all of these are deeply interrelated in actual lived experience. He cites contemporary cognitive science to argue that even the lowest-level perceptions are "in general simultaneously conceptions." Here is where much white ignorance has its roots, shaping even most basic perceptions of privileged perceivers in ways that block access to certain kinds of knowledge.[6] In the case of race, this is augmented by "white normativity," that is, the taking of white lives and experience as the norm for what counts as "human" (WI 24–25), a familiar phenomenon to feminists in the form of "male normativity," for example, in the medical literature Tuana discusses. Mills's account of testimony, or the refusal to accept the testimony of oppressed groups, is similar to Tuana's account of "epistemically disadvantaged groups" (WI 31). Mills, however, is more explicit than Tuana is open about the motives behind white ignorance: white self-interest feeds and lives off of the systematic ignorance of the privileged about the lives of those they oppress (WI 34).

II

Putting epistemologies of ignorance in the broader context of ontological humility helps to answer two sorts of challenges. The first set of challenges is raised by women of color and appears, for instance, in Mariana Ortega's contribution to the *Hypatia* issue. Ortega focuses on Tuana's "loving ignorance" and raises the possibility that feminist epistemologies of ignorance, in attempting to cure such ignorance about the lives of women of color, might result in a "loving, knowing ignorance" that would only be "arrogant perception that involves self-deception and the quest for more knowledge about the object of perception . . . even though such [knowledge] claims are not checked or questioned."[7] In the Harry Potter stories, Ron opposes Hermione's efforts to free Hogwarts's house-elves by hiding knitted hats where they can pick them up, because "They should at least see what they're picking up," so the elves can make an explicit, knowing choice to be free (which they refuse).[8] A more unfortunate real world example is the Australian case discussed by Townley, which can be seen as an instance of how well-intentioned feminists can produce as much ignorance as knowledge when they study the lives of less privileged women. Such an approach would obviously perpetuate the privilege and power of white feminists without necessarily resulting in any knowledge that would benefit the women whose lives they study.

The second challenge is raised by Harvey Cormier in *Race and Epistemologies of Ignorance*. Cormier argues against Mills from a neopragmatist perspective that "After we realize that no one has access to a world beyond all of these deceptive appearances, the issue of what structures of deception are hiding that world from us will not seem urgent."[9] In Cormier's view, there is no context-free, final reality behind the "appearances" of everyday life, only those appearances themselves. His criticisms, then, is that epistemologies of ignorance seem to rely on an appearance/reality distinction that is isomorphic with the hierarchical dualisms discussed in the last chapter and therefore not ultimately sustainable. The persistence of hierarchical dualism in some discourse about epistemologies of ignorance may be due to the fact that they have their origin in feminist science studies and critical race theory, enterprises that look at the disparity between knowledge claims of dominant groups and relatively obvious scientific or social realities.

These two challenges to epistemologies of ignorance may seem to correspond to the two directions from which they have developed because Ortega's comments appear in the context of Tuana's work, Cormier's in response to Mills's. The challenges, however, are not as independent as they may look: they both warn against the dangers of a second-order epistemological arrogance, one that is possible only once one acknowledges a certain level of first-order ignorance and begins to think about the conditions of its production. On this common ground, Ortega focuses on the risk of arrogance with regard to nondominant groups, Cormier on a lingering metaphysical foundationalism he finds in Mills's work. Moreover, both challenges make equal sense when applied to either Tuana's or Mills's account of epistemologies of ignorance. Ortega, for instance, points to the reliance of white feminists who practice "loving arrogance" on "a binary system in which there is an inside/outside, a center/margin," rejecting the more complex, plural "reality" that the lives of women of color bring into focus (BLKI 71). This arrogance, then, rests on the same foundationalist certainty put into question by Cormier. Conversely, while unable to say Mills ignores the voices of people of color, Cormier does wonder how an epistemologist of ignorance "can tell *which black people* are the victims of ideology and which are not" when the argument assumes "the reality of race and race differences" (ENQ 63–64, his emphasis). His argument, like Ortega's, is that race-based power relations can still function in epistemologies of ignorance to privilege some and disadvantage others.

I bring Heidegger into the conversation to answer these challenges because his thought allows us to make distinctions among the various types of ignorance, specifically to separate those that are irreducible features of human existence, like death and language, and must be respected ("ontological" in Heidegger's sense[10]), from those that are contingent and local ("ontic" for Heidegger), and require feminist, antiracist, and generally counterhegemonic remediation. Such remediation, I will also argue, can be, in fact must be based, not on the kind of absolute ground that both Ortega and Cormier reject, but on a coherent, pluralistic, and fluid account of "reality" against which epistemologies of ignorance can measure knowledge claims.

III

As we have seen, Heidegger argues that truth (*alethēia*, what is not-forgotten) is possible only on a background of what is forgotten or unknown. This means that our knowledge depends in important ways on what is implicitly known but cannot necessarily be made explicit—background assumptions, practical skills, cultural understandings, and so forth. Moreover, we cannot explicitly know everything at the same time. Thus, what we can't know shapes the outline and provides the supporting framework for what we can. This means that for Heidegger, truth is context-dependent and largely contingent, rather than certain and universal, because it depends on preexisting knowledge and current conditions of knowledge acquisition. It is only the specific material circumstances of Professor Trelawney's predictions (primarily tone of voice) that allow Harry and Dumbledore to pick the rare genuine prophecies from her usual sham. These background conditions include what Tuana calls the "practices" of knowledge production, and they function at a variety of levels—individual, local, social, and material—without ever being the objects of explicit attention, or critical scrutiny. Heidegger claims that it is only on the basis of this implicit background of un-truth or concealment that explicit truth claims can become "unconcealed."

From this two things follow. First, all epistemologies are epistemologies of ignorance, that is, all knowledge claims conceal as much as they reveal, including the conditions of their own production and the power relations they serve. This affirms Ortega's concern that even feminist epistemologies of ignorance can become arrogant by pointing out that they are no different in essence from any other epistemology. Second, what is concealed, the background, is itself context-dependent and contingent, reliant on further (if not necessarily deeper) background conditions of equal complexity. What makes one claim more true than another is not "conformity" to things for Heidegger, but the way in which it serves the "true" needs of a particular historical time and place. But, Cormier would point out, what can this last "true" mean, if there is no longer any absolute foundation? Only, for Heidegger, that in addition to what it "unconceals," the truth also points to all that it must leave hidden. The solution to "arrogant" ignorance is not more valid testing against a fixed reality, but an openness to the possibility of error and a recognition of the limits of human knowing. Just as a work of art should reveal its own status as a work for Heidegger, truth should reveal its own status as contingent and partial.

Most feminists and others doing work on epistemologies of ignorance know this. What Heidegger adds is a broader philosophical basis that both explains the importance of this intellectual enterprise, and allows us to refine our understanding of epistemologies of ignorance in Tuana and Mills's more narrow sense. Heidegger suggests an ontological epistemology of ignorance, an analysis of the absolute limits of human knowledge. Any given case of ignorance, especially of the kind of concern here, however, will have an "ontic," that is, concrete, contingent history that allows us to distinguish between ignorance induced by unavoidable limits (the absence of telescopes, say) and ignorance that conceals what could, under different conditions governed by different power relationships, be revealed (such as still believing in a geocentric theory of the universe in Europe after 1700).

Note that there are two dimension of analysis here that cut across each other to create different three dimensions of critique. One dimension is how open a particular set of knowledge practices is to the possibility of basic error in its operations, and how adequately it acknowledges its own limitations. The second dimension is the one just noted—the reliance of knowledge practices on power relations to undergird the truths they produce. Galileo was not necessarily less arrogant in the first sense than the Pope because he probably believed he had discovered an absolute truth, but his claims about the solar system didn't require the power of the papacy to be recognized by his peers as more true than the Church's version. On the other hand, the reliance on power to enforce knowledge claims is inherently incompatible with an understanding of Heidegger's ontological point because it relies on claims of fixed, foundational knowledge to justify ignoring what could otherwise be known.

This resolves Cormier's problem in a way that avoids some forms of relativism. White ignorance about the history, lives, contributions, and so on, of black people and other people of color is not due primarily to background conditions, but is refutable by historical, sociological, and other facts of a sort that the same ignorant white knowers would accept in other knowledge contexts. What medical science doesn't know about the clitoris can be resolved without reference to a "reality" of the human body beyond the "reality" that guides other investigations into human physiology. Knowledge is contextual, but we have a well-established context for judging questions like these against which white ignorance or medical ignorance can be measured, not absolutely, but within the same confines as we determine the role of protein in cell development or how the steam engine transformed British life.

This answers Cormier by making it clear that the issue of which "structures of deception are hiding" a supposedly fixed reality seems "urgent," not because epistemologies of ignorance necessarily posit such a reality, but because they approach the problem as a question of political praxis. If we adopt this view, the "victims of ideology" he refers to are those who change their view of what constitutes a good argument when they move into areas of race, gender, and other forms of domination. (Similar epistemic errors are constantly made in the Harry Potter books by the great masses of witches and wizards who want only to be reassured and rely for their information on the <u>Daily Prophet</u> and the Ministry of Magic.) This view is enriched by Tuana's account of the creation of "epistemically disadvantaged identities," which offer as an additional measure of any truth claim the extent to which the voices of all those in a position to know were heard in determining that "truth."

We can see, then, that feminist, antiracist, or other counterhegemonic epistemologies of ignorance run two risks. The first is the one noted by Ortega, the risk of conflating "ontic," remediable ignorance with, as Tuana says, "what we cannot know." Failing to see this distinction can lead to attempts to create knowledge about the lives of others that ignores what it is ignorant of, that is, the knowledge those others have about their own lives. The other risk, reiterating in another way Cormier's point, is the danger of thinking that epistemologies of ignorance, with their focus on what we don't know, describe something different from any other account of knowledge. If one might reasonably object to Heidegger's "Truth, in its essence, is un-truth" (BW 179), I would argue that it is far harder to deny that knowing, in its essence, is not (fully) knowing. The arrogance to be feared is not only of the "loving" sort Ortega warns us against that wants to know more than it can about the Other, but also of the ontological sort Cormier hints at, an arrogance that already claims to know more than it can, one that pretends to offer solutions to unsolvable conditions of human life.

Humility Beyond the Divides: Race/Gender

binary thinking: a system of thought that divides concepts into two oppositional categories, for example, white/black, man/woman, heterosexual/homosexual, saint/sinner, reason/emotion, and normal/deviant.

—Patricia Hill Collins, *Black Sexual Politics*

I

Epistemological concerns are also a major focus in Patricia Hill Collins's influential *Black Feminist Thought* (1990). In her conclusion to that book, she notes several points on which an Afrocentric feminist epistemology would diverge from traditional philosophical accounts of knowledge, while at the same time maintaining "points of contact" with both feminist and Afrocentric perspectives. She believes that maintaining these contacts is important because it "challenges additive analyses of oppression claiming that Black women have a more accurate view of oppression than do other groups." Her concern is that gender and race oppression be seen as intersecting dimensions in the lives of Black[11] women that create a uniquely Black feminist standpoint that cannot be placed in a hierarchical relationship with the knowledge claims of other groups.

According to Collins, the key features of Black feminist thought include a clear distinction between knowledge and wisdom, and "the use of experience as the cutting edge dividing them." "Knowledge is adequate for the powerful," she notes, "but wisdom [based on experience] is essential to the survival of the subordinate." She also identifies this as one point of contact with African-American thought and with women's ways of knowing in general: "Some feminist scholars offer a similar claim that women as a group are more likely than men to use concrete knowledge in assessing knowledge claims."[12] Another trait that she identifies in Black feminist epistemology is the use of dialogue to validate knowledge claims (an emphasis it apparently shares with Socrates and Plato). "For Black women new knowledge claims are rarely worked out in isolation from other individuals and are usually developed through dialogues with other members of a community." She says that this practice has Afrocentric roots, and distinguishes it from the adversarial debate that is the paradigm in most contemporary philosophical discourse (BFT 212), but links the practice again to feminist epistemology.

The final trait that is relevant here is what she calls "an ethic of personal accountability." She explains by saying that "African-Americans reject the Eurocentric, masculinist belief that probing into an individual's personal viewpoint is outside the boundaries of discussion. Rather, all views expressed and actions taken are thought to derive from a central set of core beliefs that cannot be other than personal" (BFT 218). It is the purported "objectivity" of the media and the ability of its writers, such as Rita Skeeter, to say something one day and deny it the next that allows the *Daily Prophet* to become a propaganda arm of the Ministry of Magic, and ultimately of Voldemort's Death Eaters. Collins notes in her book that the connection between this awareness of the power relations that underlie and can distort knowledge claims and feminist views at the time is less clear, but it should be obvious from the previous section that feminist epistemology has in fact evolved in this direction over the time since Collins's book appeared, at least in part due to her work.

Collins herself is an example of how "Black feminist thought demonstrates Black women's emerging power as agents of knowledge." She believes her work and the work of other Black feminists makes two major contributions to our understanding of the relationship between knowledge and power. First, it provides new paradigms and allows us to see all forms of oppression as parts "of one overarching structure of domination" (BFT 221–222). The second major contribution follows from the fact that

> Black women have not conceptualized our quest for empowerment as one of replacing elite white male authorities with ourselves as benevolent Black female ones. Instead, African-American women have overtly rejected theories of power based on domination in order to embrace an alternative vision of one based on a humanist vision of self-actualization, self-definition, and self-determination. (BFT 224).

She also argues that an interlocking model of oppression, as opposed to an additive one, helps to undermine the hierarchical dualisms that, as we have already seen, dominate the philosophical tradition, and opens space for a "both/and conceptual stance" (BFT 225).

The paradigm shifts Collins describes adds a further complication to our conceptual schemes because Black feminist thought reveals that domination, and resistance, can happen on three interrelated levels: the level of personal experience, the level of community, and the level of social institutions (BFT 227). Another kind of complication is the fact that the connections Black feminist thought maintains with feminism and an Afrocentric standpoint can also be sources of tension and conflict. For instance, "Those Black women who are feminists are critical of how Black culture and many of its traditions oppress women. . . . But these same women may have a parallel desire as members of an oppressed racial group to affirm the value of that same culture and traditions" (BFT 231–232). These tensions create a Black feminist standpoint that is particularly well situated to generate ontological humility. "No one group has a clear angle of vision. No one group possesses the theory or methodology that allows it to discover the absolute 'truth' or, worse yet, proclaim its theories and methodologies as the universal norm evaluating other groups' experiences" (BFT 235). At the same time, Collins believes Black feminist thought can create not only new knowledge, but also a new politics of power.

II

Collins begins *Black Sexual Politics* (2005) with a reminder that "knowledge and power are deeply linked, and achieving social justice requires attending to both."[13] The subtitle of this book refers to a "new racism," which she characterizes as carrying forward many dimension of the "old" racism, but with new features such as heavy reliance on mass media to spread its ideology and the controlling image of Black youth as at risk or as "the problem," in a new context of globalization and the increasing power of trans- and supernational corporations (BSP 54). Another feature of this new racism is "color-blindness," defined in the glossary as "a racial ideology that gained prominence during the post–civil rights era that argues that using racial language perpetuates racism" (BSP 349). (Consider again the color- and gender-blindness in Harry Potter's world.) The result of the new configurations of race domination is that "The joblessness, poor schools, racially segregated neighborhoods and unequal public services that characterize American society vanish, and social class hierarchies in the United States, as well as patterns of social mobility within them, become explained solely by issue of individual values, motivation, and morals" (BSP 178). At the same time, in keeping with her earlier work, she underscores the fact that "African American men and women both are affected by racism, but in gender-specific ways" (BSP 5).

The focus in this book, however, is clearly on politics, and specifically sexual politics. After noting that "gender" is not all about women because "Men's experiences are also deeply gendered," and that "Sexuality is not simply a biological function; rather, it is a system of ideas and social practices that is deeply implicated in shaping American social inequalities," she defines "sexual politics" as "a set of ideas and social practices shaped by gender, race, and sexuality that frame all men and women's treatment of one another, as well as how individual men and women are perceived and treated by others." Moreover, "Because African Americans have been so profoundly affected by racism, grappling with racism occupies a prominent place within Black sexual politics" (BSP 6). She also says explicitly in her Introduction that she offers few solutions to the problems she describes because "becoming empowered means learning how to think for ourselves and making decision that are in our own best interests," and she invites "non-African American readers to consider how the questions raised here might inform their own social justice projects" (BSP 9). She also reasserts the view that all forms of social domination are "mutually constructed systems of power" (BSP 11).

In contrast to what we saw earlier in Foucault, she worries that "the rush to abandon the black/white paradigm of race in the United States in favor of other seemingly more universal paradigms potentially distorts the uniqueness of African American struggles and can also support new forms of racism" (BSP 12). She is open, however, about the connections between her work and Foucault's. "In order to prosper," she says, for instance, "systems of oppression must regulate sexuality" (BSP 36). Like Derrida, she notes with regard to words such as *jungle*, *primitive*, and *wild* that "history hides in the shadows of these terms, because these concepts are incomprehensible without a social context giving them meaning" (BSP 42). She adds that "ideologies of all sorts are . . . always internally inconsistent" (BSP 314). In addition to using the binaries of hierarchical dualism quoted above as an explanatory category, she raises a point that will be developed in the next section, that "Within white/black binary thinking, ideas about racial normality and deviancy draw heavily upon ideas about gender and sexuality for meaning." For this reason, she argues, "The refusal to discuss *in public* the profound influence of Western constructions of a deviant Black sexuality on African American men and women leaves a vacuum in contemporary African American sexual politics" (BSP 44–45, her emphasis).

Echoing, from another perspective, aspects of the work of both Foucault and Heidegger, she underscores that "Contemporary forms of oppression do not routinely force people to submit. Instead, they manufacture consent for domination so that we lose our ability to question and thus collude in our own subordination. . . . [O]ppression becomes expressed as a routinized violence or normalized war within our society." This violence can be overt, but "also operates in the infra-politics of everyday life, through a series of mini-assaults that convince each one of us to stay in our place" (BSP 50–51). She reviews much of the history we will see in the next section, declaring that "the past is ever present," and points out that "In the United States, the assumption that racism and homophobia constitute two separate systems of oppression masks how each relies upon the other for meaning" (BSP 88). This is because in a system governed by hierarchical dualisms, "installing White heterosexuality as normal, natural, and ideal requires stigmatizing alternate sexualities as abnormal, unnatural, and sinful" (BSP 97). The paradoxical logic of hierarchical dualism that we found in Derrida is obvious here as well: "African Americans are counseled . . . to believe that, although these [White, heterosexual] gender roles may be more difficult for African Americans to attain, such roles are nonetheless natural and normal" (BSP 183).

III

On this basis, Collins is able to develop a theory of Black sexual politics that has the potential to create a new political vision while also tacitly encouraging the ontological humility of the actions and practices that might arise from it. For example, she notes that in most Black discourse about the lynchings of the Jim Crow era, "race and gender constituted separate rather than intersecting forms of oppression that could not be equally important" (BSP 216), rather than regarding "institutionalized lynching and [the] rape [of Black women by White men] as *different* expressions of the *same* type of social control" that would "strip victims of agency and control over their own bodies, thus aiming for psychological control via fear and humiliation" (BSP 218, her emphasis). More generally, she argues, rape and the persistent threat of rape connect "sexuality and violence as a very effective tool to routinize and normalize oppression" (BSP 232). Furthermore, "Because these practices are implemented by large, allegedly impartial bureaucracies, the high incarceration rates of Black men and the use of capital punishment on many prisoners becomes seen as natural and normal" (BSP 232–233). Such insights, then, can become focal points for understanding the pragmatic importance of a new Black sexual politics.

This politics connects with an antihomophobic politics through the recognition that "People who are alienated from one another and from their own honest bodies become easier to rule" (BSP 249). Given the power of the governing images of female desirability and Black women in our culture, "For heterosexual African American men, *choosing to love and commit to a heterosexual relationship with a Black woman is a rebellious act.*" So, too, are homosexual love relationships, if for obviously different reasons. However, rebelling "simply against the rules" is not enough. We must also rebel "against what the rules are designed to do [which] creates space for a very different set of individual relationships, and a more progressive Black sexual politics" (BSP 250–251, her emphasis). Black love relationships of all kinds must contest the dominant culture discourse because "manipulating sexuality, annexing the power of the erotic, and using both to deny the very humanity of love constitute important mechanism of social control." She cites Paul Gilroy, who suggests that "because literal freedom has been won, Blacks search for substantive freedom by escaping into personal relationships and striving for freedom via the release provided by sexual orgasms." Collins argues against this that "this interior space of sexuality, sensuality, the erotic, and love, does not always serve as a dense transfer point of power that disempowers African American men and women" (BSP 293–295).

Buried deep in the endnotes to her book, however, is one of the most interesting analyses Collins offers. She comments that because the rhetoric of color-blindness challenges White supremacy, "it make color-blindness 'doubly difficult to contest.'" Collins cites a study of White supremacist discourse by Abby L. Ferber,[14] who found that "race and gender differences are constructed as hierarchical and necessary. Thus, efforts to erase hierarchy are reinterpreted as efforts to do away with racial and/or gender differences." For example, allowing same-sex marriage attacks the dualisms on which the institution of marriage is based (male/female, virtue/sin, etc.), and so, the argument against it goes, would erase all differences and allow marriage between more than two people, with animals, and so forth. "At the same time," Collins goes on, "the framework of [color-blind] equality provides no space . . . for bona fide 'differences' that can be used to remedy past and present inequalities. The result is an *impotent* antiracist and feminist discourse that is trapped between tenets of White supremacy and a head in the sand color blindness" (BSP 331, my emphasis). The perverse logic of merely reversing hierarchical dualisms is such that "The total absence of black people would signal the failure of color blindness," so "color blindness" requires an invisible Blackness because one can only be blind to what, in fact, actually exists (BSP 178). Even in Rowling's color-blind world, the only ethnicities identifiable at Hogwarts are those attributed to people of color, Professor McGonagall, and a single Irish student.

Collins admittedly offers more questions than answers. Starting with the claim that "Within the confines of race, African Americans police one another, using the cross-cutting weapons of sexuality, gender, and class," she asks "Is it possible to craft a new gender ideology, new understandings of Black sexuality, and new social class relations that are not predicated on dominance?" Her answer seems in many ways merely to restate the question in the positive:

> Black people must rebel against existing Black sexual politics throughout the entire system; from the micro-politics that frame the one-on-one interactions of everyday life, through trying to change the ethos of the Black Church and other Black community organizations; through the macro-politics of building new social movements with other groups who are engaged in similar social justice initiatives.

The hows remain unclear. Still, to explain "the connections among soul, spirituality, embodiment, sexuality, expressiveness, eroticism, and sexuality" she thinks are vital to Black sexual politics, she quotes a passage from James Baldwin that mixes desire and transcendence in an ontological humility clearly echoed in Collins's own work: " 'To be with God is really to be involved with some enormous, overwhelming desire, and joy, and power which you cannot control, which controls you' " (BSP 295).

Beyond the Divides: Race/Sexuality

> [The leaders of the black civil rights movement] are American heroes. . . . They weren't perfect—except in little sparks from time to time—and they didn't always know whether what they were doing was right. They just did their best.
>
> —Ladelle McWhorter, *Racism and Sexual Oppression in Anglo-America*

I

To move from Collins's books to Ladelle McWhorter's *Racism and Sexual Oppression in Anglo-America* takes us backward in historical time, because McWhorter investigates how racism and homophobia developed in tandem as new and powerful tools of domination from the earliest days of United States history. McWhorter begins with a warning similar to Collins's: "laxity about differences between social movements, histories, and bigotries is dangerous."[15] She argues, however, that race and sexuality "are historically codependent and mutually determinative. Approaching them separately therefore insures that we will miss their most important features" (RSO 14). An endnote to this passage refers to the similarity between her project and Collins's, but notes that Collins "offers a rather different analysis than the one I will offer here" (RSO 335). One major difference is that McWhorter rejects the analytic concept of intersectionality that Collins believes is so useful, because McWhorter thinks it oversimplifies the interactions between various forms of oppression and focuses too much on identities and not enough on institutions and discourse. McWhorter also thinks the concept suggests more independence in the operations of twentieth-century racism, sexism, and heterosexism than she believes exists (RSO 15).

She begins with the quotation from Foucault discussed earlier, that the development of psychiatry as a profession gave rise to a "racism against the abnormal" and contrasts his willingness to "draw on the history of oppression of nonwhite peoples to illuminate the suffering of non-heterosexual (and other 'non-normal') people of all colors and ethnicities" with her own reticence, as a Lesbian in the United States, about making the same intellectual move (RSO 32). She interprets Foucault's comment as saying that within racist "regimes of power," the objects of racism are considered "abnormal" in some way and that "abnormality" is in fact one major reason "they are despised, excluded, contained, managed, or exploited." She agrees in many ways with this claim—"Modern racism is about racial purification. . . . Modern racism is not really about nonwhites; modern racism is all about white people," just as the "racism" in Rowling's saga is all about pure blood witches and wizards. McWhorter then traces the history of the English word *racism* back to its origin in anti-Nazi discourse in the mid-1930s, when it was applied only to individuals and their beliefs. Not until the mid-1960s did leaders in the black power movement use the word to describe institutions (RSO 34–37). The history of the word leads McWhorter to conclude that "the word *racism* has become a political flashpoint loaded with connotation but lacking any stable referent at all . . ." (RSO 41).

McWhorter cites Foucault's genealogy of the term "race war,"[16] revealing that it first appears in the 1630s, "when various factions in English society . . . claimed that the Stuart monarchy was illegitimate," so from the beginning the term was connected to conflict and power relations, if of an unexpected sort (RSO 57). In this early context, "race" meant a lineage of European people, such as Saxons or Normans or Scots (or "pure bloods"), but McWhorter notes that "Race war discourse is a powerful way of dividing an 'us' from 'them,' whoever us and them may be" (RSO 60). She says that Foucault came to believe that "biopower" (which McWhorter defines as "vast, growing, and intensely interconnected networks of normalizing discourse and practices" [RSO 54]) and racism were inextricably linked. "Biopower can't function without racism, and modern racism takes shape within the forces of biopolitical function and expansion" (RSO 58). In her book, she traces the lines of the convergence between biopower and racism in the history of the American colonies after 1700, not as a challenge to Foucault's claim, but as "refinements and supplementations" (RSO 62). In so doing, however, the ontological humility of her own approach underscores again how necessary it is in our attempts to theorize about oppression in the contemporary world.

II

In the history McWhorter traces, we learn that slavery in the American colonies was not initially based on race, since English indentured servants worked side by side with slaves imported from Africa. Neither was slavery motivated by "racism"—the main motive was profit (RSO 70). The first "race," in the contemporary sense, to be defined was the white race, which

> was established as a legal and economic category in colonial, then in U.S. law and policy as a way of co-opting the European-American portion of the labor force . . . so that enslavement of a subset of the total labor force—the African American portion—could proceed unhampered . . . [T]he invention of the white race was, in effect, the invention of morphological race itself. (RSO 72–73)

By "morphological race," McWhorter means "race" as based on how people look, rather than on what we would now call their ethnic heritage, such as Saxon, Norman, or Scots. She traces the development of this concept to a series of laws passed in the Virginia Colony starting in 1705. Only later did this political use of "morphological race" become influential in the thinking of European scientists about biology and heredity.

Another main turning point in this history is when two lines of thought, race and biological kinds, begin to converge with evolutionary theory and changes in normalizing discourse about madness and idiocy. This last then led to the concept of the "moral idiot" who lacked any ability, or desire, to make correct moral choices, which in turn created a pragmatic concern with female "moral idiots," who were likely to produce more of the same kind and to spread venereal disease, then incurable and a major public health problem (RSO 134). By the end of the nineteenth century, the list of evolutionary "degenerates" had grown to include "Imbeciles, criminals, prostitutes, consumptives, Africans, Asians, Mexicans, Jews, Irishmen, masturbators, deaf-mutes, epileptics, psychopaths, and shiftless Appalachian paupers," all of whom, despite the obvious differences between them, "posed a serious threat to the continued purity" of the white (Northern European) "race," which was seen as the apex of human evolution. "This," she explains, "is scientific racism," more preoccupied with protecting the race that "matters" than with attacking other races. Not, of course, that its effects didn't result in the oppression of other races. But McWhorter's focus at this point is scientific racism insofar as it "attempted to control and enhance every aspect of human reproduction and sexuality," that is, insofar as it was part of "a regime of biopower" (RSO 139–140).

The homosexual remains hidden in the above list of degenerates under the label "the masturbator," but McWhorter's genealogy reveals "the story of how the figure of the homosexual arose within the same racist scientific discourses and science-influenced social practices and [shows] the close kinship between the myths of the black rapist and the homosexual predator" (RSO 142). She recounts, as does Collins, the horrific history of lynchings in the United States and the evolution of the myth of the black rapist, but also a parallel history of sexuality that transforms the masturbator into the preying homosexual. This shift was facilitated by the fact that in the nineteenth-century "masturbation" included "mutual masturbation and oral sex" (RSO 184). The problem with such people, from the perspective of the nineteenth century, was that, beyond the "immoral acts" in which they engage, they could "induce perversion" in others, that is, as McWhorter puts it, "sexual inverts recruit." Worse, "A surprising number of white women were vulnerable to same-sex seduction," thus putting the white race once again at risk (RSO 186–187). The black rapist and the homosexual predator alike were "the haunting presence of the savage ancestor, the bestial atavism, the throwback to an uncivilized past. They had no place in that bright and shining future that evolution promised" (RSO 194). Therefore, they had to managed, confined, or killed.

The ideology of evolution and race in this period took a unique form in the U.S., not only because of slavery, but also because the nation could not be identified with any "living race." "It was a legal rather than an historic and organic unity . . ." (RSO 198). In response, American political and scientific discourse about race tended to see Anglo-Americans (outside Appalachia) as identical with the white race, "the Race," per se (RSO 202). This led to massive regulation of American life to protect "the Race" through limitations on immigration and marriage, lifelong commitment of the insane, sterilization of poor and nonwhite women, the death penalty, and extensive reliance on intelligence and psychological testing. These normalizing discourses, McWhorter goes on to explain, both created and relied on a governing image of the "normal" American family as under attack by the "deviant" families created in nonwhite communities and by "deviant" sexualities. Eventually, this led to Federal Bureau of Investigation director J. Edgar Hoover's 1937 declaration of "War on the Sex Criminal," but McWhorter suggests that "the all-out persecution of homosexuals began at the national level" in 1950 with the McCarthy hearings that identified homosexuals as traitors in the Cold War era (RSO 275). At the same time, the relatively new science of sociology was beginning to "discover" what Daniel Patrick Moynihan would later call the "pathology" of the black family (RSO 288).

It is in this context that McWhorter agrees with Foucault: "contemporary racism, the racism that arose in the twentieth century as heir to scientific racism and racist eugenics, is racism against the abnormal." (The depth of this racism in our world is echoed in the title of the pamphlet Harry Potter sees being collated in the last book of the saga: "MUDBLOODS and the Dangers They Pose to a Peaceful Pure-Blood Society.") For McWhorter, however, this claim is not an arrogant assertion of the primacy of abnormality over other pretexts for oppression, but the door to a profound racio-ontological humility. If this is true, she says, "racism looms much larger and goes much deeper in our national and our personal lives than even the most racially aware and sensitive among us might think. It structures our educational institutions; . . . it shapes our self-perceptions as well as our perceptions of every person we meet. Our halls of justice reverberate with it." This is a racism of abnormality, she argues, because while we may refuse to see members of any racial group as inferior, we do believe that "abnormality *does* equal inferiority, that abnormal people are inferior to normal people, and that many abnormalities . . . *are* reliable indicators of moral worth." The challenge McWhorter sets for us is to ask how to "dismantle *that* racism" (RSO 291–292, her emphasis).

III

As with Collins, there are more questions here than answers, but McWhorter does make a few concrete suggestions. She joins Foucault (and Collins, Tuana, Mills, etc., as well as, implicitly, Rowling) in asserting the importance of "subjugated knowledge" that has been buried and disqualified as knowledge by the dominant discourse because it generates a genealogy of struggles. She also emphasizes the epistemological humility of her own position: "I have not presented a story of the development of modern racism in these pages that claims to be *the* definitive, final account as over against false accounts already circulating." She claims merely to have made "the question of what racism is, where it comes from, and what it allies itself with too complex and too persistent and too frightening to put down," calling her work, therefore, "an act of philosophy." Feminism is largely tacit here, but she has "attempted to de-subjugate and incite feminist knowledge and queer knowledge of sexuality's intimate connection with white supremacy." And she does draw some conclusions, including that "the only way to fight racism successfully is to critique and displace officially recognized antiracist discourses simultaneously" in what Derrida might call a double movement of deconstruction (RSO 295–296).

Constantly aware of the unique history of black people in the United States—she notes that "To distort or obscure a history that an oppressed group has lived through is, whether one means to or not, to exercise domination over that group" (RSO 317)—she draws her vision of a possibly better world from the black civil rights movement of the 1960s, and specifically the vision of Dr. Martin Luther King, Jr. "It was a vision of a world without rank," she says, without violence. "It was a vision antithetical to the picture of the world inherent in disciplines of normalization, management and control" or, in Heidegger's terms, to the possibility of humans as standing reserve (RSO 321). Conversely, she warns us, "when any group of people decides it is more important to assert their normality and beg for acceptance than to assert their freedom and demand respect on their own terms, the battle for justice and equality is already lost" (RSO 323). She argues that "We who are oppressed in various ways must assert our equality—that is, we must proclaim and bear in our comportment the fact that we *deserve* the respect and consideration of our neighbors and fellow citizens," but not in arrogant self-assertion. Rather, "we have to assume responsibility for our lives and our communities" (RSO 325, her emphasis).

Two of her additional recommendations for how to combat racism and other forms of biopower are especially important here. The first is that we must "refuse to do the work of self- (and other-) policing in the name of the normal." The second is that, as epistemologies of ignorance tell us, "we must *know*—actively and adamantly—*what we know*." Part of Harry Potter's battle is to accept and insist on what he knows from his own experience, against the supposed knowledge of others, and above all to name the enemy. In contrast to Foucault's focus on the impersonal domination of biopower, she especially urges us to acknowledge what we know about those who would oppress us:

> that their allegedly rational and disinterested justifications for their actions are rooted in a desire for material gain and a drive for territorial and political hegemony that spans four centuries of industrial development and brutal conquest, and that the allegedly objective natural and social sciences they tout were conceived and expounded in service to the racist goal of Anglo-Saxon domination.

A final recommendation is to "stop compartmentalizing oppression on the basis of sociological identity," although she agrees "Identity politics may well have its place." The most important thing is to be aware of is that "nobody is normal, and nobody ought to be" (RSO 326–328, her emphasis).

Conclusion

It's a cold and it's a broken hallelujah . . .
—Leonard Cohen, "Hallelujah"

With the discussion of race in Collins and McWhorter, we have come full circle to Rowling's assertion that an antiracist moral stance is at the core of the Harry Potter saga. It should be clearer now how ontological humility, and its other, are systematically tied to, without being confined to, the dynamics of race in the modern world. Racism, in both its U.S. and Nazi forms, can in fact be understood as a direct refusal of ontological humility in reaction to historical forces (e.g., lack of identity as a nation, long-standing religious prejudice, the humiliation of the Versailles Treaty) that bring the demand for such humility to the forefront of a people's consciousness. Of course, there are other factors, above all economic ones, that contribute to such manifestations of human arrogance, but tied to a tradition more open to ontological humility (one thinks of the Danish or the Dutch in World War II), their effects can be less devastating. So the literary conclusion here, if you will, is that arrogance and humility constitute a largely implicit, or "unthought" in Heidegger's sense of the term, theme in the Harry Potter books, which underlies the Rowling's explicit antiracism. As already noted, Rowling certainly marks arrogance as a profound and disturbing evil when it does raise its head in her saga: "[Harry] could not lie to himself; if he had known the prefect badge was on its way, he would have expected it to come to him, not Ron. Did this make him as arrogant as Draco Malfoy? Did he really think himself superior to everyone else?"[1]

Philosophically, however, what Rowling (along with a few other popular authors of magical tales in the last century, such as C. S. Lewis, J. R. R. Tolkien, and T. H. White[2]) may have done is to make more explicit a theme that has, as I've argued, run through the work of major European philosophers for at least the last 400 years without ever being labeled as such. Still, it could be argued that some of the philosophers discussed here were to some extent aware of their own ontological humility, albeit not under that name, and that of others—one might see this kind of awareness as what drew, for instance, Kant to Hume or Heidegger to Kierkegaard. So why does ontological humility remain only implicit in their work? Why don't these philosophers label it, explain their reasons for it, engage others in philosophical exchanges about it? Why does ontological humility reappear over and over again in the history of philosophy, only to vanish and need to be re-created in each new generation of philosophers?

I think one answer to this question may lie in the word "humility." Aristotle already considered "undue humility" a vice for those he taught (although probably not for women and slaves), and the Christian virtue of humility could be said to fall closer to that end of the spectrum than to the end represented by the justified (and hence often limited) ambition that I argued earlier may play the role of ontological humility for Aristotle. Annette Baier offers one version of the contemporary attitude toward Christian humility when she says, somewhat scornfully, that it "can scarcely be thought to pass the test of reflection" (HRWE 28), because it creates the paradox of a demand to be humble about one's humility. This, of course, again confuses personal humility, of which this may be true, and ontological humility, of which I would argue it is not. In any case, we inherit from two millennia of Christianity a concept of humility that is nearer to servility than Kantian wonder. Given that, and our culture's even longer obsession with an individualist model of masculinity with its roots in honor, pride, and physical strength, why would any man, outside of the confines of certain forms of religious life, want to flaunt his humility, much less recommend it to others as a virtue? What kind of scorn would a man who preached or promoted humility have been subject to? (Kierkegaard might be a useful example here.) One profound link between ontological humility and feminism is that in our culture humility remains powerfully culturally coded as feminine, so to articulate it as a philosophical view is to become in some sense, as Baier said of Hume, "a virtual woman."

But if generations of great philosophers, for whatever reason, either missed the call to ontological humility or failed to develop it fully as a philosophical view, how can an understanding of ontological humility be gleaned from reading something like the Harry Potter saga? Clearly, Rowling being a woman is not enough to explain turning the "base" metal of a story for children into philosophical gold. Despite its brilliance and amazing popularity, like Lewis's, Tolkien's, and White's stories, Rowling's book remains "genre fiction," popular fiction of a particular type (science fiction, fantasy, detective fiction, romance, cowboy stories) that is identified primarily by its relatively predictable plot and inevitable happy ending (or at least the vanquishing of evil), but above all by its "failure" to be literary fiction.

As we enter the realm of literature, however, it is important to note the intimate connection Heidegger makes between what he calls "poetry" and the unthought. At the end of "The Origin of the Work of Art," he says that "Poetic projection comes from nothing in this respect, that it never takes its gift from the ordinary and traditional. Yet it never comes from nothing in that what is projected by it is only the withheld determination of historical Dasein itself" (OWA 200). That is, art brings into the open the unthought of the world created in that open. Aeschylus's "Eumenides" makes explicit the waning of the power of the female-identified Furies in favor of the male-identified goddess Athena. Velázquez's *Las Meniñas* marks the end of the reign of the king and the beginning of the reign of "man." Melville's *Moby Dick* brings to light the dark fear of a world without God that marked the last decades of the nineteenth century.

Those works, however, are "great" art—literary fiction and painting in their highest forms. And the argument here has not been that the Harry Potter saga "attains to its historical essence as foundation" (OWA 201), as Heidegger says of the works of art he addresses. Still, we have seen that Rowling's books, again like Lewis's, Tolkien's, and White's, reveal one piece, perhaps one important piece, of the unthought of the modern world in a way that makes it available to those who have never studied great works of art or walked into a philosophy classroom. This may be the role of the best genre art—to bring to everyone the insights philosophy and literary fiction may bring to only a few.[3] And Rowling's saga has the advantage for the new century of putting the emphasis on a form of ontological arrogance, racism, that is both broader and more deeply rooted in our culture than the nationalism more appropriate to the conflicts of the mid-twentieth century. Rowling's world is not Britain in the past or the future, but the global world of our technological present, and, while racism may not be the only or perhaps the most dangerous form of arrogance in that world, it is at least one that opens the window to the underlying error of believing that humans can know everything, do anything, and control their own destiny.

From the most abnormal of wizards, who must battle not only pure arrogant evil but also the arrogant normalizing practices of the Ministry of Magic, to McWhorter's declaration of the impossibility, and even undesirability, of human normality, ontological humility provides a continuous critical counterpoint to the dominant discourses, not only of Western philosophy but of the culture at large over at least the last four centuries. Ontological humility allows us to see beyond claims of certain knowledge, whether based on reason or on science; provides a basis for challenging the environmental degradation and other excesses of the technological age; helps us live lives of existential authenticity; reveals structures of domination; explains our ignorance as well as our knowledge; and suggests how we might better share the world across the boundaries of gender, race, sexuality, ethnicity, social class, age, nationality, and religion. It tells us why we find some philosophers dark and draining to read and others, whose ideas are no less deep and complex, invigorating and life-affirming. Kierkegaard complains that nineteenth-century philosophy "is unwilling to stop with doubting everything but goes further" in an attempt to reach total knowledge of God and the world, whereas the ancient Greeks assumed doubt—genuine questioning of the ground of our existence—"to be a task for a whole lifetime" (FTR 5–6). In the twenty-first century, I would ask what philosophy might be if it rethought the possibility of that "everything" and began, not with doubt, but with the gratitude of the ancient Greeks, and with ontological humility.

Notes

Prologue: Defining Ontological Humility

1. David Hume, *An Enquiry Concerning Human Understanding*, ed. Eric Steinberg (Indianapolis: Hackett, 1977); hereafter cited as ECHU with a page reference.
2. Søren Kierkegaard, *Fear and Trembling with Repetitions*, trans. Howard V. and Edna H. Hong (Princeton, NJ: Princeton University Press, 1983), pp. 1–123; hereafter cited as FTR with a page reference.
3. Marilyn Frye, "In and Out of Harm's Way: Arrogance and Love," *The Politics of Reality* (Trumansburg, NY: The Crossing Press, 1983), pp. 52–83; hereafter cited as AL with a page reference.
4. This is not the case, for instance, in J. R. R. Tolkien's *The Lord of the Rings*, where Sauron's evil is often evoked, but no claim is ever made that he might have broken something like "rules" governing his magic.
5. Martin Heidegger, *Basic Writings*, ed. David Farrell Krell (San Francisco: Harper, 1993), pp. 238–239; hereafter cited as BW with a page reference.
6. J. K. Rowling, *Harry Potter and the Order of the Phoenix* (New York: Scholastic Books, 2003), pp. 842–843.
7. J. K. Rowling, *Harry Potter and the Half-Blood Prince* (New York: Scholastic Books, 2005), p. 33.
8. J. K. Rowling, *Harry Potter and the Order of the Phoenix*, p. 670.
9. J. K. Rowling, *Harry Potter and the Half-Blood Prince*, pp. 36–37.
10. J. K. Rowling, *Harry Potter and the Half-Blood Prince*, p. 623.
11. J. K. Rowling, *Harry Potter and the Deathly Hallows* (New York: Scholastic Books, 2007), p. 563.
12. Aristotle, *Nicomachean Ethics*, trans. David Ross (New York: Oxford University Press, 1980), 1123a–b.
13. Martin Heidegger, *The Question Concerning Technology*, trans. William Lovitt (New York: Harper, 1977), p. 116; hereafter cited as QT with a page reference.

On how our (potential) omniscience came to replace God's, see also Michel Foucault's *Las Meniñas* in *The Order of Things*, trans. unattributed (New York: Vintage, 1973).

14. J. K. Rowling, *Harry Potter and the Chamber of Secrets* (New York: Scholastic Books, 1999), p. 314.

15. J. K. Rowling, *Harry Potter and the Goblet of Fire* (New York: Scholastic Books, 2000), p. 653.

16. J. K. Rowling, *Harry Potter and the Deathly Hallows*, p. 708.

17. J. K. Rowling, *Harry Potter and the Order of the Phoenix*, p. 784.

18. J. K. Rowling, *Harry Potter and the Sorcerer's Stone* (New York: Scholastic Books, 1997), p. 291.

19. J. K. Rowling, *Harry Potter and the Order of the Phoenix*, p. 127.

20. Lorraine Code, "Skepticism and the Lure of Ambiguity," *Hypatia*, vol. 21, no. 3 (Summer 2006): 222–228; hereafter cited as SLA with a page reference.

21. This difference will be discussed more fully in the next chapter, but it is worth noting that there is a middle position that shows up in some versions of American Pragmatism. The sometimes extremely subtle difference between Pragmatism and analytic philosophy, between Pragmatism and what Code calls Continental philosophy, and even among the Pragmatists themselves, however, would constitute too long a detour to permit a fuller explanation here.

22. A. J. Ayer, *Language, Truth and Logic* (New York: Dover, 1952), p. 32.

23. Robert R. Ammerman, ed. *Classics of Analytic Philosophy* (Indianapolis: Hackett, 1990), p. 2.

24. J. K. Rowling, *Harry Potter and the Deathly Hallows* (New York: Scholastic Books, 2007), p. 563.

25. Reprinted in Naomi Scheman, *Engenderings* (New York: Routledge, 1993), pp. 245–249.

26. J. K. Rowling, *Harry Potter and the Goblet of Fire*, p. 110.

27. Susan Bordo, *The Flight to Objectivity* (Albany, NY: State University of New York Press, 1987).

For another, nonfeminist, version of this argument with Heideggerian overtones, again, see Michel Foucault, *The Order of Things*.

28. On this see, for instance, Evelyn Fox Keller's classic *Reflections on Science and Gender* (New Haven, CT: Yale University Press, 1985).

29. Much has, of course, already been done to open it to feminist analysis from within Heidegger's own tradition. See, for example, *Feminist Interpretations of Martin Heidegger*, eds. Nancy J. Holland and Patricia Huntington (University Park, PA: Penn State Press, 2001).

30. See his "Letter on Humanism" in *Basic Writings*, in note 5, cited above.

31. On this see, again, Evelyn Fox Keller, *Reflections on Science and Gender*.

32. CNN's international branch is heavily supported by nations proudly advertising to American and European businesses the high educational level of their citizens and the low wages they can be paid.

33. See Meditation Four, "this reason suffices to convince me that the species of cause termed final, finds no useful employment in physical [or natural] things; for it does not appear to me that I can without temerity seek to investigate the [inscrutable] ends of God." (*The Philosophical Works of Descartes*, trans. Elizabeth S. Haldane and G. R. T. Ross [Cambridge: Cambridge Uni-

versity Press, 1911], I-173; hereafter cited as PWD with a volume number and a page reference)

34. Thomas Kuhn, *The Structure of Scientific Revolutions* (Chicago: University of Chicago Press, 1970). See also Michel Foucault, *The Order of Things*, cited above.

35. On this, see also Bruno Latour, *We Have Never Been Modern*, trans. Catherine Porter (Cambridge, MA: Harvard University Press, 1993).

36. Søren Kierkegaard, *Either/Or, Volume I*, trans. David F. Swenson and Lillian Marvin Swenson and *Either/Or, Volume II*, trans. Walter Lowrie (Princeton, NJ: Princeton University Press, 1959).

37. *Harry Potter and the Deathly Hallows*, pp. 212–214.

Harry's arguments here may fall within the Ethical, too, but are of a different order, emphasizing family relationships rather than abstract duty. For more on the feminist implications of this inversion of Socrates's argument in Plato's "Crito," see Nancy J. Holland, "The Opinions of Men and Women: Toward a Different Configuration of Moral Voices," *The Journal of Social Philosophy*, vol. 24, no. 1 (Spring 1993): 65–80.

38. Aristophanes, "The Clouds," trans. Peter Meineck, in *The Trials of Socrates*, ed. C. D. C. Reeve (Indianapolis: Hackett, 2002).

39. Gabriel Marcel, *Being and Having*, trans. unattributed (New York: Harper, 1965), p. 15; hereafter cited as BH with a page reference.

40. Jean-Luc Nancy, *The Experience of Freedom*, trans. Bridget McDonald (Stanford, CA: Stanford University Press, 1993), p. 20; hereafter cited as EF with a page reference.

41. The French *l'étant* is much less used than the English *being*, and so carries both more emphasis and more technical philosophical connotations. Although it begs several questions in the interpretation of Nancy's text that are not directly relevant to the present discussion, I have capitalized the *B* in this quotation for clarity and consistency.

42. For a more detailed account of this connection, which comes into the tradition from Kant, see the next chapter.

Chapter One: Epistemological Humility and Its Other

1. J. K. Rowling, *Harry Potter and the Deathly Hallows* (New York: Scholastic Books, 2007), p. 153.

2. Thomas Hobbes, *Leviathan*, ed. Curley (Indianapolis: Hackett, 1994), p. 74.

3. See, for instance, Susan Bordo, *The Flight to Objectivity*, p. 108, and Naomi Scheman, *Engenderings*, p. 67.

4. Whether Descartes is correct in this interpretation of Aristotle's concept of a final cause is a separate question that we won't be able to address here.

5. J. K. Rowling, *Harry Potter and the Sorcerer's Stone*, p. 254.

6. As my colleague Stephen Kellert reminds me, while this may be the popular understanding of modern science, the contrast between the reality of current scientific practice and alchemy may not be as clear cut as suggested here.

7. Genevieve Lloyd, *The Man of Reason: "Male" and "Female" in Western Philosophy* (Minneapolis: University of Minnesota Press, 1984).

8. David Hume, *A Treatise of Human Nature*, ed. L. A. Selby-Bigge (Oxford: Oxford University Press, 1975), p. 1; hereafter cited as THN with a page reference.

9. David Hume, *Dialogues Concerning Natural Religion and the Posthumous Essays*, ed. Richard H. Popkin (Indianapolis: Hackett, 1980), pp. 95–95; hereafter cited as DCNR with a page reference.

10. John Locke, *An Essay Concerning Human Understanding*, ed. John W. Yolton (New York: Dutton, 1972), vol. 1.

11. See, for instance, Baruch Spinoza, *The Ethics and Selected Letters*, trans. Samuel Shirley, ed., Seymour Feldman (Indianapolis: Hackett, 1982), parts III and IV.

Descartes, of course, also wrote "Passions of the Soul" near the end of his life at the urging of Princess Elizabeth, but his English editors indicate a certain reluctance on his part to have it published (PWD II-330).

12. The limitations of the fact/value distinction on which much of Hume's moral philosophy rests will be discussed in the next chapter.

13. For Mill's version, see John Stuart Mill, *Utilitarianism*, ed. George Sher (Indianapolis: Hackett, 2001).

14. David Hume, *Hume's Enquiries*, ed. L. A. Selby-Bigge (Oxford: Oxford University Press, 1975), p. 215; hereafter cited as HE with a page reference.

15. Annette Baier, "Hume: The Women's Moral Theorist?," *Women and Moral Theory*, Eva Feder Kittay and Diana T. Meyers, ed. (Totowa, NJ: Rowman & Littlefield, 1987), pp. 37–55.

16. Annette Baier, "Hume: The Reflective Women's Epistemologist," *Feminist Interpretations of David Hume*, Anne Jaap Jacobson, ed. (University Park, PA: Penn State Press, 2000), pp. 19–38; hereafter cited as HRWE with a page reference.

17. Richard Popkin, "Editor's Introduction," DCNR, xv. See also Prologue, p. 26, above.

18. Jacques Derrida, as we will see, might make much of this doubly attenuated location for such a major claim.

19. Immanuel Kant, *Prolegomena to Any Future Metaphysics*, trans. Paul Carus, revised by James W. Ellington (Indianapolis: Hackett, 1977), p. 5; hereafter cited as PAFM with a page reference.

20. See, for instance, J. K. Rowling, *Harry Potter and the Prisoner of Azkaban*, p. 129.

21. Rae Langton, *Kantian Humility: Our Ignorance of Things in Themselves* (Oxford: Clarendon Press, 1998).

22. Immanuel Kant, *Grounding for the Metaphysics of Morals*, trans. James W. Ellington (Indianapolis: Hackett, 1981), p. 46; hereafter cited as GMM with a page reference.

23. For a fuller discussion of this problem in Kant, see Nancy J. Holland, *The Madwoman's Reason: The Concept of the Appropriate in Ethical Thought* (University Park, PA: Penn State University Press, 1998), pp. 44–57.

24. Immanuel Kant, *Critique of Practical Reason*, trans. Lewis White Beck (New York: MacMillan, 1956), p. 77; hereafter cited as CPR with a page reference.

Chapter Two: Ontological Humility in Heidegger

1. Martin Heidegger, *Phenomenological Interpretations of Aristotle*, trans. Richard Rojcewicz (Bloomington, IN: Indiana University Press, 2001), p. 28.

2. Heidegger borrows the term from G. W. F. Hegel, but tracing the connection between the two uses of the term would be too long a detour to take here.

3. J. K. Rowling, *Harry Potter and the Deathly Hallows*, p. 759.

4. Martin Heidegger, *Being and Time*, trans. James Macquarrie and Edward Robinson (New York: Harper, 1962), p. 188; hereafter cited as BT with a page reference.

5. Jean-Luc Nancy discusses this aspect of Heidegger's thought in the chapter of *The Experience of Freedom* on evil (EF 121–141), but most explicitly in his footnotes (EF 200 n 3 and 201–202 n 11).

6. Martin Heidegger, *Plato's Sophist*, trans. Richard Rojcewicz and André Schuwer (Bloomington, IN: Indiana University Press, 1997), p. 24; hereafter cited as PS with a page reference.

7. An example of this was a recent television commercial that referred to cell phones outside the reach of their network as in "paperweight" mode, or as merely present-at-hand objects in this way.

8. J. K. Rowling, *Harry Potter and the Sorcerer's Stone*, p. 82.

9. J. K. Rowling, *Harry Potter and the Sorcerer's Stone*, p. 81.

10. J. K. Rowling, *Harry Potter and the Order of the Phoenix*, p. 791.

11. Plato, *Five Dialogues*, trans. G.M.A. Grube (Indianapolis: Hackett, 1981), p. 17; "See whether you think all this is pious is of necessity just."

12. Plato, *Sophist*, trans. Nicholas P. White (Indianapolis: Hackett, 1993), p. 39.

13. In fact, the glossary in Heidegger's *Plato's Sophist* gives "presence" as the first definition for "*energeia*," but that seems to beg far too many questions; "actuality" is listed in the glossary to *Aristotle's Metaphysics* Θ *1–3* (see note 15).

14. For a more technical and detailed version of this argument, see my "Rethinking ecology in the Western philosophical tradition: Heidegger and/on Aristotle," *Continental Philosophy Review*, vol. 32, no. 4 (October 1999): 409–420.

15. Martin Heidegger, *Aristotle's Metaphysics* Θ *1–3*, trans. Walter Brogan and Peter Warnek (Bloomington, IN: Indiana University Press, 1995); hereafter cited as AM with a page reference.

16. The translators of *Aristotle's Metaphysics* chose to use "being" for the German "das *Sein*" where the translators of the other of Heidegger's works cited used "Being" (AM, xii); I will insert the capital *B* where needed for consistency and clarity.

17. Compare Hume's *An Enquiry Concerning Human Understanding*, pp. 42–46.

18. Martin Heidegger, *Parmenides*, trans André Schuwer and Richard Rojcewicz (Bloomington, IN: Indiana University Press, 1992), pp. 3–4; hereafter cited as P with a page reference.
19. Compare the discussion of the same point with regard to Aristotle, pp. 55–56 above.
20. This is Heidegger's example.
21. J. K. Rowling, *Harry Potter and the Order of the Phoenix*, p. 302.
22. J. K. Rowling, *Harry Potter and the Deathly Hallows*, p. 470.
23. Martin Heidegger, *On Time and Being*, trans. Joan Stambaugh (New York: Harper, 1972), pp. 55–57; hereafter cited as TB with a page reference.
24. Martin Heidegger, *On the Way to Language*, trans. Peter D. Herta (New York: Harper, 1971).

Chapter Three: Existential Humility and Its Other

1. Jean-Paul Sartre, *Being and Nothingness*, trans. Hazel Barnes (New York: Pocket Books, 1966); hereafter cited as BN with a page reference.
It may be worth noting that the years in which the books by the French existentialists were first published probably don't reflect in any exact way the years in which they were written, since many were written during the Nazi occupation of Paris, when publication was difficult, if not impossible.
2. Jean-Paul Sartre, *Essays in Existentialism*, ed. Wade Baskin (New York: Citadel, 1988), pp. 36–38; hereafter cited as EE with a page reference.
3. For Genet's own story, see Jean Genet, *The Thief's Journal*, trans. Bernard Frechtman (New York: Grove Press, 1964). For Sartre's interpretation, see Jean-Paul Sartre, *Saint Genet, Actor and Martyr*, trans. Bernard Frechtman (New York: Braziller, 1963).
4. Simone de Beauvoir, *The Second Sex*, trans. Constance Borde and Sheila Malovany-Chevallier (New York: Knopf, 2009).
5. Albert Camus, *The Myth of Sisyphus and Other Essays*, trans. Justin O'Brien (New York: Vintage, 1983), pp. 13–15; hereafter cited as MS with a page reference.
6. Simone de Beauvoir, *The Ethics of Ambiguity*, trans. Bernard Frechtman (New York: Citadel, 1976), pp. 7–10 (my emphasis); hereafter cited as EA with a page reference.
Please note that, as mentioned above, like English and unlike German, French provides Beauvoir with no way simple gender-neutral way to refer to humans collectively, leaving her only the conventional "man."
7. Note, however, that Merleau-Ponty expresses reservations about the word "consciousness." See Maurice Merleau-Ponty, *Phenomenology of Perception*, trans. Colin Smith (New York: Routledge, 1962), footnote p. 258; hereafter cited as PP with a page reference.
8. See Dorothea Olkowski, and Gail Weiss, eds., *Feminist Interpretations of Maurice Merleau-Ponty* University Park, PA: Penn State Press, 2006.

9. For a more detailed argument for this point, see the discussion of Merleau-Ponty in Nancy Holland, *Is Women's Philosophy Possible?* (Totowa, NJ: Rowman & Allenheld, 1990).

10. Maurice Merleau-Ponty, *The Visible and the Invisible*, trans. Alphonso Lingis, ed. Claude Lefort (Evanston, IL: Northwestern University Press, 1968), p. 3; hereafter cited as VI with a page reference.

Chapter Four: Postmodern Humility and Its Other

1. Michel Foucault, *The Order of Things*. The quoted words are the title of a subsection of chapter 9 (OT 307).

2. Michel Foucault, *Discipline and Punish: The Birth of the Prison*, trans. Alan Sheridan (New York: Vintage, 1979), p. 16; hereafter cited as DP with a page reference.

3. For a more detailed discussion of this concept in Foucault, see Nancy J. Holland, "Truth as Force: Michel Foucault on Religion, State Power, and the Law," *The Journal of Law and Religion*, vol. XVIII, no. 1 (2002): 79–97.

4. Michel Foucault, "The Subject and Power," Afterword, in *Michel Foucault: Beyond Structuralism and Hermeneutics*, Hubert L. Dreyfus and Paul Rabinow (Chicago: University of Chicago Press, 1982), p. 216; hereafter cited as MF with a page reference.

5. Michel Foucault, *The History of Sexuality, Volume I: An Introduction*, trans. Robert Hurley (New York: Pantheon, 1978), pp. 10–11; hereafter cited as HS with a page reference.

6. Michel Foucault, *Abnormal: Lectures at the Collège de France 1974–75*, trans. Graham Burchell (New York: Picador, 2003), pp. 316–317. Cited in Ladelle McWhorter, *Racism and Sexual Oppression in Anglo-American* (Bloomington, IN: Indiana University Press, 2009), p. 32.

7. His role in the publication of the memoirs of Herculine Barbin is not necessarily an exception to this. See Herculine Barbin, *Being the Recently Discovered Memoirs of a Nineteenth-Century French Hermaphrodite*, trans. Richard McDougall (New York: Pantheon, 1980).

8. For a similar argument about Foucault's work in different terms, see Jacques Derrida, "Cogito and the History of Madness," in *Writing and Difference*, trans. Alan Bass (Chicago: University of Chicago Press, 1978), pp. 31–63.

9. Jacques Derrida, "Tympan," *Margins: Of Philosophy*, trans. Alan Bass (Chicago: University of Chicago Press, 1982), pp. 327–330; hereafter cited as M with a page reference.

10. Jacques Derrida, *Glas* (Paris: Éditions Galilée, 1972).

11. Jacques Derrida, "Living On: *Border Lines*," trans. James Hulbert, *Deconstruction and Criticism*, Harold Bloom et al. (New York: Seabury, 1979).

12. Jacques Derrida, *The Post Card: From Socrates to Freud and Beyond*, trans. Alan Bass (Chicago: University of Chicago Press, 1987).

13. J. K. Rowling, *Harry Potter and the Chamber of Secrets*, p. 329 (her emphasis).

14. Jacques Derrida, *Of Grammatology*, trans. Gayatri Spivek (Baltimore, MD: The Johns Hopkins University Press, 1976), p. 18 (his emphasis); hereafter cited as OG with a page reference.

15. Jacques Derrida, *Memoirs of the Blind: The Self-Portrait and Other Ruins*, trans. Pascale-Anne Brault and Michel Naas (Chicago: University of Chicago Press, 1993), p. 127; hereafter cited as MB with a page reference.

16. Jacques Derrida, *The Gift of Death*, trans. David Willis (Chicago: University of Chicago Press, 1995), p. 45; hereafter cited as GD with a page reference.

17. See, for example, Aristotle, *Nicomachean Ethics*, trans. David Ross (New York: Oxford University Press), 1155a.

18. Jacques Derrida, *The Politics of Friendship*, trans. George Collins (New York: Verso, 1997), p. 13; hereafter cited as PF with a page reference.

19. Jacques Derrida, *Of Hospitality*, trans. Rachel Bowlby (Stanford, CA: Stanford University Press, 2000), p. 15; hereafter cited as OH with a page reference.

20. For a more detailed feminist account, see "'With Arms Wide Open': Of Hospitality and the Most Intimate Stranger" (*Philosophy Today*, vol. 45, no. 5 [SPEP Supplement 2001]): 133–137.

21. Jacques Derrida, *Paper Machine*, trans. Rachel Bowlby (Stanford, CA: Stanford University Press, 2005), p. 79); hereafter cited a PM with a page reference.

Chapter Five: Feminist Humility

1. A more developed version of this section appeared as "If I Know I *Can* Be Wrong" in *Philosophy Today*, vol. 54 (SPEP Supplement 2010): 122–127.

2. Nancy Tuana, "The Speculum of Ignorance: The Women's Health Movement and Epistemologies of Ignorance," *Hypatia: A Journal of Feminist Philosophy*, vol. 21, no. 3 (Summer 2006): 1–19; hereafter cited as SI with a page reference.

3. J. K. Rowling, *Harry Potter and the Deathly Hallows*, p. 709.

4. Cynthia Townley, "Toward a Revaluation of Ignorance," *Hypatia: A Journal of Feminist Philosophy*, vol. 21, no. 3 (Summer 2006): 37–55.

5. Charles W. Mills, "White Ignorance," in *Race and Epistemologies of Ignorance*, eds. Shannon Sullivan and Nancy Tuana (Albany, NY: State University of New York Press, 2007), p. 13; hereafter cited as WI with a page reference.

6. See also Marilyn Frye's "In and Out of Harm's Way: Arrogance and Love," cited in Prologue, note 3.

7. Mariana Ortega, "Being Lovingly, Knowingly Ignorant: White Feminism and Women of Color," *Hypatia: A Journal of Feminist Philosophy*, vol. 21, no. 3 (Summer 2006): 63; hereafter cited as BLKI with a page reference.

8. J. K. Rowling, *Harry Potter and the Order of the Phoenix*, p. 255.

9. Harvey Cormier, "Ever Not Quite: Unfinished Theories, Unfinished Societies, and Pragmatism," in *Race and Epistemologies of Ignorance*, eds. Shannon Sullivan and Nancy Tuana (Albany, NY: State University of New York Press, 2007), p. 73; hereafter cited as ENQ with a page reference.

10. This is, obviously, a much more controversial claim than I can justify here. For a fuller understanding of the complexities, see Jacques Derrida's "*Geschlecht:* Sexual Difference, Ontological Difference," in *Feminist Interpretations of Martin Heidegger*, eds. Nancy J. Holland and Patricia Huntington (University Park, PA: Penn State Press, 2001), pp. 53–72; and Elizabeth Grosz's "Ontology and Equivocation: Derrida's Politics of Sexual Difference," in *Feminist Interpretations of Jacques Derrida*, ed. Nancy J. Holland (University Park, PA: Penn State Press, 1997), especially p. 97.

11. In this section and the next I will following the conventions used by the respective authors for "Black" and "White," both of which Collins capitalizes and McWhorter does not.

12. Patricia Hill Collins, *Black Feminist Thought: Knowledge, Consciousness, and the Politics of Empowerment* (New York: Harper, 1990), pp. 207–210; hereafter cited as BFT with a page reference.

13. Patricia Hill Collins, *Black Sexual Politics: African Americans, Gender, and the New Racism* (New York: Routledge, 2005), p. 3; hereafter cited as BSP with a page reference.

14. Abby L. Ferber, *White Man Falling: Race, Gender, and White Supremacy* (Lanham, MD: Rowman & Littlefield, 1998).

15. Ladelle McWhorter, *Racism and Sexual Oppression in Anglo-America: A Genealogy* (Bloomington, IN: Indiana University Press, 2009), p. 10; hereafter cited as RSO with a page reference.

16. Michel Foucault, *Society Must Be Defended: Lectures at the College de France 1975–76*, trans. David Macey (New York: Picador, 2002).

Conclusion

1. J. K. Rowling, *Harry Potter and the Order of the Phoenix*, p. 166.

2. I am thinking of Lewis's Perelandra series (especially *That Hideous Strength*) as well as his Narnia books (especially *The Voyage of the Dawn Treader*), Tolkien's stories of Middle Earth, and White's *The Once and Future King* and *The Book of Merlin*.

3. For a more complete account of genre fiction, see my "Seeing the Same World Differently: Genre Fiction and 'The Origin of the Work of Art,'" *Philosophy and Literature*, vol. 26, no. 1 (April 2002): 216–223.

Bibliography

Ammerman, Robert R., ed. *Classics of Analytic Philosophy*. Indianapolis: Hackett, 1990.
Aristophanes. "The Clouds," trans. Peter Meineck, in *The Trials of Socrates*, ed. C. D. C. Reeve. Indianapolis: Hackett, 2002.
Aristotle. *Nicomachean Ethics*, trans. David Ross. New York: Oxford University Press, 1980.
Ayer, A. J. *Language, Truth and Logic*. New York: Dover, 1952.
Barbin, Herculine. *Being the Recently Discovered Memoirs of a Nineteenth-Century French Hermaphrodite*, trans. Richard McDougall. New York: Pantheon, 1980.
de Beauvoir, Simone. *The Ethics of Ambiguity*, trans. Bernard Frechtman. New York: Citadel, 1976.
———. *The Second Sex*, trans. Constance Borde and Sheila Malovany-Chevallier. New York: Knopf, 2009.
Bloom, Harold, Paul de Man, Jacques Derrida, Geoffrey Hartman, and J. Hillis Miller, *Deconstruction and Criticism*. New York: Seabury, 1979.
Bordo, Susan. *The Flight to Objectivity*. Albany, NY: State University of New York Press, 1987.
Camus, Albert. *The Myth of Sisyphus and Other Essays*, trans. Justin O'Brien. New York: Vintage, 1983.
Code, Lorraine. "Skepticism and the Lure of Ambiguity." *Hypatia*, vol. 21, no. 3 (Summer 2006): 222–228.
Collins, Patricia Hill. *Black Feminist Thought: Knowledge, Consciousness, and the Politics of Empowerment*. New York: Harper, 1990.
———. *Black Sexual Politics: African Americans, Gender, and the New Racism*. New York: Routledge, 2005.
Derrida, Jacques. *The Gift of Death*, trans. David Willis. Chicago: University of Chicago Press, 1995.
———. *Glas*. Paris: Éditions Galilée, 1972.
———. *Margins: Of Philosophy*, trans. Alan Bass. Chicago: University of Chicago Press, 1982.
———. *Memoirs of the Blind: The Self-Portrait and Other Ruins*, trans. Pascale-Anne Brault and Michel Naas. Chicago: University of Chicago Press, 1993.

———. *Of Grammatology*, trans. Gayatri Spivek. Baltimore, MD: The Johns Hopkins University Press, 1976.

———. *Of Hospitality*, trans. Rachel Bowlby. Stanford, CA: Stanford University Press, 2000.

———. *Paper Machine*, trans. Rachel Bowlby. Stanford, CA: Stanford University Press, 2005.

———. *The Politics of Friendship*, trans. George Collins. New York: Verso, 1997.

———. *The Post Card: From Socrates to Freud and Beyond*, trans. Alan Bass. Chicago: University of Chicago Press, 1987.

———. *Writing and Difference*, trans. Alan Bass (Chicago: University of Chicago Press, 1978.

Descartes, René. *The Philosophical Works of Descartes*, trans. Elizabeth S. Haldane and G. R. T. Ross (in two volumes). Cambridge: Cambridge University Press, 1911.

Dreyfus, Hubert L., and Paul Rabinow. *Michel Foucault: Beyond Structuralism and Hermeneutics*. Chicago: University of Chicago Press, 1982.

Ferber, Abby L. *White Man Falling: Race, Gender, and White Supremacy*. Lanham, MD: Rowman & Littlefield, 1998.

Foucault, Michel. *Abnormal: Lectures at the Collège de France 1974–75*, trans. Graham Burchell. New York: Picador, 2003.

———. *Discipline and Punish: The Birth of the Prison*, trans. Alan Sheridan. New York: Vintage, 1979.

———. *The History of Sexuality, Volume I: An Introduction*, trans. Robert Hurley. New York: Pantheon, 1978.

———. *The Order of Things*, trans. unattributed. New York: Vintage, 1973.

———. *Society Must Be Defended: Lectures at the College de France 1975–76*, trans. David Macey. New York: Picador, 2002.

Frye, Marilyn. *The Politics of Reality*. Trumansburg, NY: The Crossing Press, 1983.

Genet, Jean. *The Thief's Journal*, trans. Bernard Frechtman. New York: Grove Press, 1964.

Martin Heidegger. *Aristotle's Metaphysics Θ 1–3*, trans. Walter Brogan and Peter Warnek. Bloomington, IN: Indiana University Press, 1995.

———. *Basic Writings*, ed. David Farrell Krell. San Francisco: Harper, 1993

———. *Being and Time*, trans. James Macquarrie and Edward Robinson. New York: Harper, 1962.

———. *On Time and Being*, trans. Joan Stambaugh. New York: Harper, 1972.

———. *On the Way to Language*, trans. Peter D. Herta. New York: Harper, 1971.

———. *Parmenides*, trans André Schuwer and Richard Rojcewicz. Bloomington, IN: Indiana University Press, 1992.

———. *Phenomenological Interpretations of Aristotle*, trans. Richard Rojcewicz. Bloomington, IN: Indiana University Press, 2001.

———. *Plato's Sophist*, trans. Richard Rojcewicz and André Schuwer. Bloomington, IN: Indiana University Press, 1997.

———. *The Question Concerning Technology*, trans. William Lovitt. New York: Harper, 1977.

Hobbes, Thomas. *Leviathan*, ed. Curley. Indianapolis: Hackett, 1994.
Holland, Nancy J., ed. *Feminist Interpretations of Jacques Derrida*. University Park, PA: Penn State Press, 1997.
———. "If I Know I Can be Wrong." *Philosophy Today*, vol. 54 (SPEP Supplement 2010): 122–127.
———. *Is Women's Philosophy Possible?* Totowa, NJ: Rowman & Allenheld, 1990.
———. *The Madwoman's Reason: The Concept of the Appropriate in Ethical Thought*. University Park, PA: Penn State University Press, 1998.
———. "The Opinions of Men and Women: Toward a Different Configuration of Moral Voices." *The Journal of Social Philosophy*, vol. 24, no. 1 (Spring 1993): 65–80.
———. "Rethinking Ecology in the Western Philosophical Tradition: Heidegger and/on Aristotle." *Continental Philosophy Review*, vol. 32, no. 4 (October 1999): 409–420.
———. "Seeing the Same World Differently: Genre Fiction and 'The Origin of the Work of Art,'" *Philosophy and Literature*, vol. 26, no. 1 (April 2002): 216–223.
———. "Truth as Force: Michel Foucault on Religion, State Power, and the Law." *The Journal of Law and Religion*, vol. XVIII, no. 1(2002): 79–97.
———. "'With Arms Wide Open': Of Hospitality and the Most Intimate Stranger." *Philosophy Today*, vol. 45, no. 5 (SPEP Supplement 2001): 133–137.
Holland, Nancy J., and Patricia Huntington, eds. *Feminist Interpretations of Martin Heidegger*. University Park, PA: Penn State Press, 2001.
Hume, David. *Dialogues Concerning Natural Religion and the Posthumous Essays*, ed. Richard H. Popkin. Indianapolis: Hackett, 1980.
———. *An Enquiry Concerning Human Understanding*, ed. Eric Steinberg. Indianapolis: Hackett, 1977.
———. *Hume's Enquiries*, ed. L. A. Selby-Bigge. Oxford: Oxford University Press, 1975.
———. *A Treatise of Human Nature*, ed. L. A. Selby-Bigge. Oxford: Oxford University Press, 1975.
Jacobson, Anne Jaap, ed. *Feminist Interpretations of David Hume*. University Park, PA: Penn State Press, 2000.
Kant, Immanel. *Critique of Practical Reason*, trans. Lewis White Beck. New York: MacMillan, 1956.
———. *Grounding for the Metaphysics of Morals*, trans. James W. Ellington. Indianapolis: Hackett, 1981.
———. *Prolegomena to Any Future Metaphysics*, trans. Paul Carus, revised by James W. Ellington. Indianapolis: Hackett, 1977.
Keller, Evelyn Fox. *Reflections on Science and Gender*. New Haven, CT: Yale University Press, 1985.
Kierkegaard, Søren. *Either/Or, Volume I*, trans. David F. Swenson and Lillian Marvin Swenson. Beijing: China Social Sciences Publishing House, 1999.
———. *Either/Or, Volume II*, trans. Walter Lowrie. Princeton, NJ: Princeton University Press, 1959.

———. *Fear and Trembling with Repetitions*, trans. Howard V. and Edna H. Hong. Princeton, NJ: Princeton University Press, 1983.
Kittay, Eva Feder, and Diana T. Meyers, eds. *Women and Moral Theory*. Totowa, NJ: Rowman & Littlefield, 1987.
Kuhn, Thomas. *The Structure of Scientific Revolutions*. Chicago: University of Chicago Press, 1970.
Langton, Rae. *Kantian Humility: Our Ignorance of Things in Themselves*. Oxford: Clarendon Press, 1998.
Latour, Bruno. *We Have Never Been Modern*, trans. Catherine Porter. Cambridge, MA: Harvard University Press, 1993.
Lloyd, Genevieve. *The Man of Reason: "Male" and "Female" in Western Philosophy*. Minneapolis: University of Minnesota Press, 1984.
Locke, John. *An Essay Concerning Human Understanding*, ed. John W. Yolton (in two volumes). New York: Dutton, 1972.
Marcel, Gabriel. *Being and Having: An Existentialist Diary*, translation unattributed. New York: Harper, 1965.
McWhorter, Ladelle. *Racism and Sexual Oppression in Anglo-America*. Bloomington, IN: Indiana University Press, 2009.
Merleau-Ponty, Maurice. *Phenomenology of Perception*, trans. Colin Smith. New York: Routledge, 1962.
———. *The Visible and the Invisible*, trans. Alphonso Lingis, ed. Claude Lefort. Evanston, IL: Northwestern University Press, 1968.
Mill, John Stuart. *Utilitarianism*, ed. George Sher. Indianapolis: Hackett, 2001.
Nancy, Jean-Luc. *The Experience of Freedom*, trans. Bridget McDonald. Stanford, CA: Stanford University Press, 1993.
Nietzsche, Friedrich. *Beyond Good and Evil*, trans. by Walter Kaufman. New York: Vintage, 1966.
Olkowski, Dorothea, and Gail Weiss, eds., *Feminist Interpretations of Maurice Merleau-Ponty*. University Park, PA: Penn State Press, 2006.
Ortega, Mariana. "Being Lovingly, Knowingly Ignorant: White Feminism and Women of Color." *Hypatia: A Journal of Feminist Philosophy*, vol. 21, no. 3 (Summer 2006): 56–74.
Plato. *Five Dialogues*, trans. G. M. A. Grube. Indianapolis: Hackett, 1981.
———. *Sophist*, trans. Nicholas P. White. Indianapolis: Hackett, 1993.
Rowling, J. K. *Harry Potter and the Sorcerer's Stone*. New York: Scholastic Books, 1997.
———. *Harry Potter and the Chamber of Secrets*. New York: Scholastic Books, 1999.
———. *Harry Potter and the Prisoner of Azkaban*. New York: Scholastic Books, 1999.
———. *Harry Potter and the Goblet of Fire*. New York: Scholastic Books, 2000.
———. *Harry Potter and the Order of the Phoenix*. New York: Scholastic Books, 2003
———. *Harry Potter and the Half-Blood Prince*. New York: Scholastic Books, 2005.
———. *Harry Potter and the Deathly Hallows*. New York: Scholastic Books, 2007.

Sartre, Jean-Paul Sartre. *Being and Nothingness*, trans. Hazel Barnes. New York: Pocket Books, 1966.
———. *Essays in Existentialism*, ed. Wade Baskin. New York: Citadel, 1988.
———. *Saint Genet, Actor and Martyr*, trans. Bernard Frechtman. New York: Braziller, 1963.
Scheman, Naomi. *Engenderings: Constructions of Knowledge, Authority, and Privilege*. New York: Routledge, 1993.
Spinoza, Baruch. *The Ethics and Selected Letters*, trans. Samuel Shirley, ed., Seymour Feldman. Indianapolis: Hackett, 1982.
Sullivan, Shannon, and Nancy Tuana, eds. *Race and Epistemologies of Ignorance*. Albany, NY: State University of New York Press, 2007.
Townley, Cynthia. "Toward a Revaluation of Ignorance." *Hypatia: A Journal of Feminist Philosophy*, vol. 21, no. 3 (Summer 2006): 37–55.
Tuana, Nancy. "The Speculum of Ignorance: The Women's Health Movement and Epistemologies of Ignorance." *Hypatia: A Journal of Feminist Philosophy*, vol. 21, no. 3 (Summer 2006): 1–19.

Index

a priori, 39–43, 48, 76
Abraham (father of Isaac), 16–18, 104–05
"The Age of the World Picture" (Heidegger), 12, 47, 59–60, 89
alethēia, 56–57, 64, 116
ambiguity, 8–10, 19, 75–77, 80, 83, 102
Ammerman, Robert, 9
analytic, 38–39, 50
analytic philosophy/philosophers, 9–10, 27, 63, 136n21
Anglo-American philosophy. *See also* analytic philosophy, 8–10, 13, 21, 39
Angst, 17, 47, 49, 68–76 passim, 104
Aristophanes, 17
Aristotle, 6, 26, 29, 90, 132, 137n4
 in Derrida, 101–02, 105
 in Heidegger, 50–56 passim, 58, 60, 64, 139n14
arrogance, 1, 5–7, 9–11, 19, 25, 41, 44–45, 62–63, 111, 115, 118, 131, 133
arrogant eye, 10–12, 14, 30, 55
arrogant ignorance, 113, 116
authentic/authenticity, 49, 56, 72, 104, 134
Ayer, A. J., 9

Baier, Annette, 36, 43, 132
Baldwin, James, 125
Barbin, Herculine, 141

Beauvoir, Simone de, 73, 75–80, 83, 105, 140n6
Being, 15, 20, 86–87, 90, 97
 in Heidegger, 2–4, 7–8, 12, 46, 48, 50–61 passim, 64, 69, 102, 104, 139n16
Being and Time (Heidegger), 45–53, 67, 97, 101–02, 104
Berkeley, George, 32, 37, 40
Binns, Professor, 68
biopower, 90–95, 126–27, 130
Black, Sirius, 5–7, 16, 63, 71, 77, 103
body, 28, 42, 62, 73, 76, 80–86, 91–92, 94, 100
Bordo, Susan, 11, 137n3

Camus, Albert, 2, 73–77, 80, 84
causality/causal necessity, 4, 29, 31–34, 38–42, 44, 50, 55, 60, 81
centaurs, 7, 25
Code, Lorraine, 8–10, 19, 21, 36
Collins, Patricia Hill, 111, 119–25 passim, 128–29, 131, 143n11
Comte, August, 68
Continental philosophy, 8–10, 21, 39, 136n21
Cormier, Harvey, 114–18

Dark Lord, 1, 5, 7–8, 29, 46, 63. *See also* Riddle, Tom; Voldemort
Dasein, 46–55 passim, 59, 61, 64, 68–69, 98, 102, 104

Death Eaters, 1, 5, 63, 77, 119
deconstruction, 98–101 passim, 103, 109, 129
Derrida, Jacques, 2, 89, 94–109, 122, 129, 138n18, 141n8, 143n10
Descartes, René, 13, 17, 24–34, 38, 40–41, 44, 46, 48, 50, 53, 58, 60–62, 67, 69, 71–72, 83, 97, 136n33, 137n4, 138n11
différance, 96–98, 103, 105–07
dualism, 28, 41, 62, 100–02, 109, 124. *See also* hierarchical dualisms
Dufourmantelle, Anne, 107
Dumbledore, Albus, 1, 5–6, 14, 28, 38, 80, 85, 109, 112, 116
Dursley, Vernon and Petunia, 5, 76, 108

Ellison, Ralph, 113
Empiricism, 31–32, 38–39, 81
epistemologies of ignorance, 111–18
epistemology, 1, 23, 26, 28, 30, 36, 111, 116, 119–20
es gibt, 2, 4, 64
existentialism, 2, 17–19, 48–50, 67–68, 71, 73, 76, 80, 87, 90

fact/value distinction, 36, 42, 138n12
feminism/feminist, 1, 13–14, 106, 112, 114–20, 124, 129, 132, 136n29, 137n37, 142n20
feminist philosophy, 8–10, 19, 36
feminist thought, 8, 10, 80, 111, 119–21
Ferber, Abby L., 124
Filch, 7
Foucault, Michel, 2, 89–95, 97, 122, 125–26, 128–30, 135n13, 136n27, 137n34, 141n3, 141n8
foundationalism/foundationalist, 39, 115, 117
freedom, 14, 18, 20, 44, 49, 68–74, 76–80, 84, 123–24, 130

Freud, Sigmund, 97, 103, 112
Frye, Marilyn, ix, 3, 10–14, 19, 21, 30, 36, 55, 83, 111–12

gender, 1, 3, 12, 21, 51, 76, 82, 91, 94–95, 103–05, 107–08, 111, 113, 118–19, 121–24, 134, 140n6. *See also* women
Genet, Jean, 70, 72, 140n3
genre fiction, 132–33, 143n3
Gilroy, Paul, 123
goblins, 6–7, 112
God/god, 4, 6–8, 15–18, 20, 24–25, 27–29, 31–34, 37–38, 41–42, 44, 46, 50, 56, 59–60, 64, 72, 75–76, 83, 86, 89–90, 97, 105, 109, 125, 133–34, 135n13
Granger, Hermione, 40, 71, 83, 101, 113–14
Grosz, Elizabeth, 143n10

Hagrid, 7, 25, 55
Harry Potter and the Chamber of Secrets, 6, 29, 57
Harry Potter and the Deathly Hallows, 5–6, 14, 46, 84
Harry Potter and the Half-Blood Prince, 5
Harry Potter and the Order of the Phoenix, 5
Harry Potter and the Philosopher's Stone, 3
Harry Potter and the Prisoner of Azkaban, 71, 101
Harry Potter and the Sorcerer's Stone, 3, 7
Hegel, G. W. F., 16–18, 71–72, 139n2
Heidegger, Martin, 1–15 passim, 19–21, 45–65, 67–72, 75–76, 80, 86–87, 89–93 passim, 97–104, 109, 111, 115–18, 122, 130–33, 136n29, 139n2, 139n5, 139n14, 140n20, 143n10

hierarchical dualisms, 62, 99–100, 106–09, 115, 118, 120, 122, 124
Hobbes, Thomas, 24, 31–32, 35
Hogwarts, 5, 7, 14, 25, 31, 49, 71, 77, 113–14, 124
homophobia, 111, 122, 125
house elves, 6–7, 112–14
humanism, 12, 50–51, 59, 61, 68–69, 90
Hume, David, 3–4, 9, 21, 28, 30–45 passim, 48, 50–51, 55, 58, 62, 69, 75, 83–84, 97, 132, 138n12
humility, 1, 4–9, 14–15, 18–21, 23–25, 27, 34, 36–38, 41, 62–63, 78, 131–32. *See also* ontological humility
   epistemological humility, 23–24, 26, 31, 33, 36, 41, 44–45, 48, 129
Huntington, Patricia, 136n29
Husserl, Edmund, 47, 69, 101

Isaac (son of Abraham), 16–18, 104–05
infinite resignation, 3, 15, 17–19, 36
innate ideas, 31–33, 39

Kant, Immanuel, 4, 9, 16, 18–19, 37–44, 46–48, 58, 69, 75–76, 78–79, 81, 102, 132, 137n42, 138n45
Keller, Evelyn Fox, 136n28
Kellert, Stephen, ix, 137n6
Kierkegaard, Søren, 3, 15–19, 25, 37, 47, 50–51, 71, 76, 104–05, 132, 134
Knight of Faith, 15, 18, 104
Kuhn, Thomas, 13

Langton, Rae, 41
Latour, Bruno, 137n35
Leibniz, Baron von, 26
"Letter on Humanism" (Heidegger), 2, 7, 50, 97
Lewis, C. S., 131–33, 143n2

Locke, John, 32, 40
Lloyd, Genevieve, 28
Lockhart, Gilderoy, 16
Longbottom, Neville, 84
loving eye, 3, 14, 112
Lugones, María, 112
Lupin, Remus, 7, 17

Malfoy, Draco, 5, 94, 131
Marcel, Gabriel, 19–20
Margins: Of Philosophy (Derrida), 96–98, 101–03
McGonagall, Minerva, 5, 124
McWhorter, Ladelle, 111, 125–29, 131, 133, 143n11
Melville, Herman, 133
Meniñas, las (Velázquez), 89, 133, 135n13
Merleau-Ponty, Maurice, 2, 80–87, 90, 95–96, 140n7, 141n9
metaphysics, 9, 27, 30, 39, 50–52, 54, 61, 63–64, 86, 97, 101–02
Mill, John Stuart, 35, 78–79, 138n13
Mills, Charles, 112–15, 117, 129
mitigated skepticism, 3, 34, 39. *See also* skepticism
modern philosophy, 2, 23–25, 29, 54–55, 61
modernity, 7, 9, 12–14, 21, 45, 56, 59–60, 62, 89–90, 95, 103
Montaigne, Michel de, 75
morality, 4, 16, 18, 34–36, 44, 76
mudblood, 4, 6, 29, 106, 129
muggles, 2, 5, 51, 76, 83, 106

Nancy, Jean-Luc, 20, 137n41, 139n5
Newton, Sir Isaac, 26
Nietzsche, Friedrich, 7, 5, 50, 97, 108

ontological, 3, 19–20, 25, 48, 51, 78, 115, 117–18, 133. *See also* ontological humility
ontological humility, 1–6, 8–11, 14–16, 18–21, 23, 25, 27–30,

ontological humility *(continued)*
43–44, 64, 67, 71, 73, 75, 77–79, 94–95, 131–34. *See also* humility
in Derrida, 97, 101, 108–09
in feminist thought, 3, 12–14, 19, 111, 114, 120, 123, 125–26, 129
in the Harry Potter books, 5–6, 20, 64
in Heidegger, 45, 47–48, 50–52, 54–55, 58–59, 65, 67, 69
in Hume, 31–32, 34, 36, 97
in Merleau-Ponty, 80, 84–85, 87
ontology, 3, 19, 24, 27–28, 41–42, 44, 46, 48, 53
oppression, 1, 11, 28, 78, 80, 100, 103, 112, 119–20, 122–23, 125–27, 129–30
The Order of Things (Foucault), 89–90, 135n13, 136n27, 137n34
"The Origin of the Work of Art" (Heidegger), 48, 57, 61, 133
Ortega, Mariana, 114–16, 118

Parmenides, 52, 56, 58, 64, 101
Pettigrew, Peter, 57, 63
Plato, 17, 52–54, 56, 59, 119, 137n37, 139n11
Popkin, Richard, 138n17
postmodern, 80, 87, 89–90, 95
Potter, Harry, ix, 1–2, 5–6, 8–10, 14, 17–18, 23, 25, 29, 36, 40, 46, 51, 63, 70–71, 76, 81–83, 85, 105–06, 108–09, 116, 129–31, 137n37
Potter, James, 5
Pragmatism, 114, 136n21, 143n9
presence, 53, 56, 64, 82–83, 86, 96, 98–99, 101–02, 109, 128, 139n13
present-at-hand, 48, 53, 55, 64, 69, 98, 139n7
projection, 47, 51, 75, 83, 133
Protagoras, 56
pure blood, 6, 29, 126, 129

"The Questions Concerning Technology" (Heidegger), 59–60, 63, 89
Quirrell, Professor, 7, 57, 71

race, 1, 3, 111–15, 118–19, 121–28, 131, 134
racism, 6, 94–95, 121–22, 125–31, 133
Rationalism, 25, 31–32, 38
ready-to-hand, 48
Riddle, Tom, 16, 71, 98. *See also* Dark Lord; Voldemort
Rowling, J. K., ix, 1–4, 6–7, 10, 20, 28, 31, 53, 60, 62, 81, 129, 131–32

Saint-Exupéry, Antoine de, 84
Saint-Just (French revolutionary), 80
Sartre, Jean Paul, 2, 50–51, 67–73, 75–76, 80, 85, 90, 97
Schutte, Ofelia, 9
Scheman, Naomi, 10, 137n3
Science, 9, 11, 13, 23, 25–27, 41, 58–61, 64, 79, 111, 115, 117, 128, 134, 137n6
skepticism, 8–10, 19, 30, 32, 34, 38–39, 45, 62, 97. *See also* mitigated skepticism
Slytherin, Salazar, 29
Snape, Severus, 5, 7, 63, 77
Socrates, 17–18, 119, 137n37
Spinoza, Baruch, 19–20, 27, 30, 34, 38, 41, 95
standing reserve, 12, 14, 61, 63, 90, 92, 94–95, 130
Subject/subject, 20, 49, 59, 61–62, 82, 90, 92–93, 96, 98–99
subjectivity, 64, 68, 77, 93, 99
synthetic, 39, 41–43

technological, 11, 45, 58–64 passim, 89, 95, 97, 133–34
technology, 12–15, 59–63, 91–93
thrownness, 46–47, 50–51, 83
Time-Turner, 40, 101

Tolkien, J. R. R., 131–33, 135n4, 143n2
Townley, Cynthia, 112, 114
transcendence, 4, 8–9, 19, 21, 95, 125
transcendent, 4, 18, 46, 78
transcendental, 4, 6, 9, 108
Trelawney, Professor, 31, 116
Tuana, Nancy, ix, 111–18, 129

Umbridge, Dolores, 5
Utilitarianism, 36, 75, 79. *See also* Mill, John Stuart

Van Gogh, Vincent, 57
Velázquez, Diego, 89, 133
Voldemort, 1–8, 11, 17, 29, 46, 51, 57, 59, 63, 70–71, 74, 76–77, 85, 90, 97, 112, 119. *See also* Dark Lord; Riddle, Tom

Weasley, Ron, 57, 76, 114, 131
White, T. H., 131–33, 143n2
women, 10–14, 28, 36, 43, 76, 83, 91, 94, 100, 103–07 passim, 112–15, 119–24, 128, 132. *See also* gender

www.ingramcontent.com/pod-product-compliance
Lightning Source LLC
Chambersburg PA
CBHW030828230426
43667CB00008B/1427